FROM A COUNTRYMAN'S DIARY

From a
Countryman's
Diary

by

RICHARD AGNEW

Illustrated by

HILDA AGNEW

ACKNOWLEDGEMENT

Unusual Taking Times

A Nineteen Pounder from the Don

Reprinted by kind permission of

TROUT AND SALMON

Published by The Countryman Ltd

Printed by The Leagrave Press Ltd, Luton and London

Foreword

By A. R. B. Haldane, C.B.E., D.Litt.

To be invited to write the Foreword to a book written by a close friend is at once to receive a high compliment and to face a daunting task. The writer of a Foreword must avoid writing what may seem in effect to be a review of the book, or a mere catalogue of its merits, while giving in a short compass some indication of its true nature and of the delights which a reader may expect to find within its pages. He must avoid the undue intrusion of his own personality or indeed that of the Author, leaving the book in the main to speak for itself. It is at least in the knowledge of these dangers, if not equipped with the skill to avoid them, that I address myself to my task.

This is the book of a true countryman. In the opening lines of *Fly-fishing*, Lord Grey of Fallodon wrote "It would be delightful to write about pleasures, if by doing so one could impart them to others. Many of us, if we had the gift, would no doubt take the world by storm tomorrow, with an account of the delights of living in the country." The outstanding success with which Lord Grey surmounted the difficulty of conveying to others the sense of pleasure which country life and particularly fishing gave to him was certainly due to the fact that he wrote from a full heart of things which he knew and loved and in particular to his wonderful capacity for seeing and recapturing in his writing so much of natural beauty around him.

The book of which this is the Foreword seems to me to owe much of its charm to these same attributes. Whether he writes of hunting or fishing, gardening or bird-watching or simply recalls the ever-changing pageant of country life through the passing year the Author writes of scenes, episodes and activities so vivid to his mind's eye that no small part of the beauty and the pleasure which he enjoyed passes from writer to reader. Some who read the pages which follow may know little of the hunting field. To others—though these will be fewer—the delights of salmon fishing or even the simpler joys of trout fishing may be relatively rare occurrences. Many there will be who do not know the banks of the upper reaches of the Aberdeenshire Don where, as Spring passes to summer, primroses and king-cups give way to mimulus and meadow-sweet, and the banks of golden broom sweep up to the woods and the heather of the surrounding hills. But the Author has cast his net wide, and few, surely, will there be for whom these pages will not give pleasure in recalling beauty and pleasure, experienced perhaps in the very scenes of which the Author writes, perhaps more often in the woods and fields and beside the rivers of their own recollection and their own choice.

No one reading these pages can fail to realise how much the pleasure which they give is enhanced by the illustrations from the pencil of the Author's wife. Many a book on country life or country sport has been illustrated with photographs, often of high quality; but even the best photograph is a poor thing, seldom adequate to convey or illustrate the thoughts inherent in or invoked by a book of this type. The photograph is essentially concrete and realistic in character, foreign to, or even sometimes destructive of, the more abstract thoughts which line drawings or wood-cuts illustrate so well and so naturally. In the present case Author and illustrator have worked throughout in unison of thought and purpose, the work of the one complementary to that of the other. So, with text and illustrations in complete and happy harmony, I leave this book to the quiet enjoyment of the reader.

CONTENTS

Chapter		Page
1	The Countryman's Line	11
2	From our Windows	14
3	Birds in our Garden	18
4	Spaniels	32
5	Characters	50
6	An Annual Cricket Match	65
7	September Cub-hunting	72
8	Woodmen	76
9	Anecdotes	82
10	A Beginner's First Fish	88
11	Grafton Recollections	92
12	Charlton Ponds	103
13	A Pytchley Hunt	116
14	A First Point-to-Point	122
15	Hunting Reminiscences	125
16	Donside	137
17	A Nineteen-pounder from the Don	150
18	The Path through the Forest	155
19	Unusual Taking Times	158
20	Shooting over Dogs	163
21	Fishing Anecdotes	166
22	Hat-Tricks	176
23	Happy Memories	180

CHAPTER ONE

The Countryman's Line

"MY GOD what a dump!" said the taxi-driver as he helped me with my suitcases.

I must admit that at 6 o'clock on a winter evening, with the wartime black-out in force, Marylebone Station, terminus of the G.C.R., was not an inspiring sight. But that taxi-driver was quite wrong.

For many of us living in the Midlands, Marylebone was the beginning of the "Countryman's Line", and the gateway to all delights. The very names of the stations at which the train stopped en route to the heart of England, has a musical sound — Harrow-on-the-Hill — Aylesbury — Finmere — Brackley — Woodford Halse — Rugby — Lutterworth — Leicester — Loughborough — Nottingham. Could anything conjure up better the essence of the English Midlands? Visions arise of the rounded hills and wooded valleys of the Chilterns; of the great grazing grounds of the Vale of Aylesbury; of the hunting countries of Warwickshire, Northamptonshire and Leicestershire, and at the end of the journey the country of Robin Hood and Maid Marion.

It is true that in those days, fast non-stop trains ran from Marylebone even deeper into the Midlands. The "Master Cutler" and the "South Yorkshireman" were famous. But to the ordinary traveller on the "Countryman's Line" these were not really important. It was the accuracy with which they ran to time that we found so impressive. When my children were young they knew exactly where to be, and were ready at the precise moment to exchange waves with the engine driver.

Marylebone is like a country station set down in London. It is small, and in those days we knew most of the staff at least by sight. The crowded bustle of a big terminus was absent. There was an atmosphere of almost leisurely efficiency, which is not met with in many stations today. At our local station this was even more in evidence. There we knew the station staff well, and the interest on both sides was a personal one. I can remember our Station Master ringing up my wife to tell her that the London train would be half-an-hour late, so that she need not worry if I did not arrive home on time.

I often think, that on the human side, we have lost a great deal in personal contacts today. Perhaps efficiency has increased, but something has gone that will not be recovered. This does not refer only to British Railways. In the days before the telephone was automatic, we had a feeling that we knew the people personally who worked on the local exchange. I have a delightful recollection of asking for a neighbour's number, only to be told—"It is no use ringing them Sir, Mrs. B—— is hunting and the General has gone to London."

Now the "Countryman's Line" is closed, and no trains run beyond Aylesbury. Perhaps it was inevitable. Its devotees, though loyal, were few in number. A line on which one could almost count on a 3rd Class compartment to oneself, could scarcely claim that the burden of traffic made it essential. Possibly it was no more in keeping with life today than a stage coach would be. Another link with the past has been broken, and in a few years will be forgotten.

CHAPTER TWO

From our Windows

WE are extremely fortunate in having a view from the windows of our house that is particularly lovely. We overlook lawns and parkland beyond. As my wife and I are both early risers, the first thing we do is to look out of the window. Hardly a morning passes without our seeing something of interest.

The animals that come up close to the house in the early hours provide most excitement. We once looked out to see a roe-deer calmly browsing on the leaves of a cherry-tree only fifteen yards away. He appeared quite unperturbed. After a time he came closer still, before trotting off and disappearing into the shrubbery between our drive and the church. He was in no hurry, pausing now and then to nibble the grass, giving us a wonderful close up view of him.

Probably the foxes provide us with more amusement

than anything else. There is one—I always like to think that it is the same one—who behaves as though he owned the place. I have seen him sitting on the lawn completely unconcerned. I once saw him making a stalk in the rough grass beyond the lawn, then with a glance over his shoulder as much as to say—"See you again tomorrow" —he loped slowly away. I think that one year we had a litter in a big old drain under the drive. Certainly I saw two well-grown cubs playing not far away from it, but before I could get my glasses on them they had gone.

I do not care for grey squirrels. They are tree rats, and I am sure they do much harm to the nesting birds. We saw one racing along with an egg in its mouth, being attacked by two sparrows. They come on to the bird-table in winter, and that was certainly not installed for their benefit. I know they damage young trees, particularly conifers. But when there is a brood living close by, it is hard not to take a personal interest in them.

The family that live in our garden are almost white, at least they all have broad white waistcoats. The young ones are very amusing to watch as they play. In the interest of the birds, I did try to move them off by putting a shot through the drey; but it was too well tucked away in the fork of a copper beech for anything I could do to be effective. There are no red squirrels in our part of the country. It seemed odd to be told by a Scottish friend that he had never seen a grey one. I wish we could say the same thing about our spinneys.

Some mornings a hedgehog scuttles over the lawn. I like to see him, as I understand that he is a benefit to the garden. The same thing cannot be said of the moles. Not that one ever sees them, but on many mornings our first glance out of the window discloses a fresh lot of mole hills thrown up during the night.

The first sign that spring is on the way is the appearance of the snowdrops and aconites. These grow in abundance with us. Then in February come the crocuses, to be followed by the daffodils in March. We have very large numbers of daffodils and narcissi, both early and late varieties. Multi-coloured aubretia grows in masses, so that the spring provides a colourful sight.

The chief glory of the view from our windows however, is undoubtedly the trees. First in importance among these are two giant beeches and a copper beech, which at certain times of the year call for daily admiration. The beeches were carefully pollarded in early youth, and they now have a really magnificent spread. In addition to these there is a pink and a white flowering cherry, two pink horse-chestnuts, and a little farther off some fine trees of the common variety. In the distance, but near enough to display their autumn colours, are numbers of mixed hardwoods, mainly beech, in the spinneys round the park.

I find it hard to decide which season is the most attractive. Each has its own beauty. Even in winter the majesty of the bare limbs, and the tracery of the upper branches against the sky are very impressive. With the arrival of spring the trees come to life.

In April, for a short time, the beeches are a lovely

delicate green, and the young leaves on the copper beech are particularly attractive. By May all the flowering trees have come into bloom, and the mixture of colours is delightful. As summer progresses the trees lose their interest, but we have the pleasure of seeing the roses.

Then comes the splendour of the autumn. This can occur almost overnight. How long we have it, depends of course on the frosts and the wind. But sometimes for a fortnight we have a display of varying shades, the beauty of which is hard to describe. Soon after this the dark mornings are with us, and we find little to sidetrack us while dressing. From then on we are more likely to be in time for breakfast than at other seasons of the year.

We count the view from our windows one of the great attractions of our home.

CHAPTER THREE

Birds in our Garden

NEITHER my wife nor I would claim to be ornitholo-
gists, nor even bird watchers in the true sense of the
word, but we get immense enjoyment out of watching the
birds that live with us. It is very lucky for us that a good
number either reside in or visit our garden, so we feel
that we know many of them intimately.

Our house is secluded, which is a big advantage. The
layout of the garden is suited to most varieties of birds.
Directly in front of the house is a small lawn surrounded
by rose beds, which is further enclosed by rambler roses.
Beyond this enclosure lies a big expanse of lawn ending
in an area of rough grass bordering the river, and at one
end of this there is a pond. Across the stream is parkland
surrounded by spinneys. Shrubberies and pine trees grow
close up to one end of the house, while some really fine
forest trees grow within a hundred yards of it. This

diversity leads to many species breeding close at hand, so that we sometimes get the most unexpected visitors to the small lawn.

Naturally it is this part, inside the rambler fence which comes in for most observation. The bird-table stands on this small lawn. There is also a little court outside the kitchen window which is constantly under view.

We get a good dawn chorus from spring onwards, but in recent years it has not been quite as good as in the past. I do not believe that the thrushes have really recovered their numbers since the hard winter of 1962-63. It is less often now that we have one sitting on our gate post and singing to us in the evening. Any fall in their numbers would of course make a big difference. The blackbirds who fortunately are hardy enough to withstand any winter, open the morning chorus and supply most of the music.

FLYCATCHER

The summer visitors that give us most enjoyment are undoubtedly the spotted flycatchers. Quite a number of them nest with us, and one particular pair comes annually to the same place. Their first choice is a pyrecanthus on the stone pillar of our garden gate. It has happened that a robin, who claims that part of the garden as his territory, has opposed their selection of this site. Their second choice in this event is some dead ivy in the court outside the kitchen. We are quite pleased when they are denied their first selection, as we keep the creeper on that pillar carefully clipped and trained. Of course if nesting operations take place there, it has to be neglected during that period. We aim to have it well trimmed back before the time that we expect them to arrive, hoping that we shall be able to attack it again the moment the young birds have flown.

The fact that we are continually passing through the gate or working in the vicinity of the nest, appears not to worry the hen bird in the least. The only thing which seems to upset her is my straw hat! If I go through the gate wearing this she immediately leaves the nest in protest. Normally we adopt a polite fiction that neither of us is aware of the presence of the other. Possibly we stare straight at each other in passing, but as long as it does not go beyond this, and no halt is made for close inspection, honour is satisfied.

One year we had a departure from the usual sequence. In accordance with our practice, the moment the young birds had flown, we pulled out the nest and trimmed the pyrecanthus. Within a week the pair were back starting to build again. However, they did not continue for long. Whether they were annoyed at finding the remains of the old nest removed, or whether the hen decided that she did not want to go through it all again and "put her foot down", I do not know. After a day or two either they, or another pair of flycatchers, built in a clipped pyrecanthus on a wall of the house about fifty yards away. Once more they were in a position that we were continually passing; once more we had to go through the pantomime of not seeing each other, and once more we had to delay further trimming until the nesting operations were over.

If it was the same pair that we had watched on the pillar, they must have found the new site far less satisfactory, as the wall faced south and we were having a spell of hot weather. After the young ones were hatched we saw the hen on several occasions sitting gasping on the edge of the nest sheltering them from the sun. Nevertheless, all went well, the young brood flying off early in August.

The swallows and martins nest in a number of places close to the house. Fortunately for us many of them select the telephone line as a suitable resting place during the first flight of the young birds. This wire is under close observation from a bathroom window. I regret to say we spend a lot of time that could no doubt be more usefully employed, watching the proceedings.

Five or six young birds sit along the line while the hen flies in every minute or two to feed them. This goes on for some little time, then she varies her tactics. Instead of delivering the food she flies in close, but at the last moment, swings away leaving a line of gaping mouths and disappointed faces behind her. When this has happened two or three times "the penny drops"—the young birds take off after her, and another brood is launched.

GREAT TIT   COAL TIT   BLUE TIT

In winter the bird-table gives us endless enjoyment. Needless to say it is usually the property of the great and blue tits, but the coal tit is also a frequent visitor. He has a reputation for being shy, but we have not found this to be the case. The nuthatch is a regular caller.

NUTHATCH

When he comes he arrives like a dive bomber and everybody else has to make way. Incidentally, at one nesting time a nuthatch decided that the best way by which he could get cement to build up his nest was to take it from between the bricks of our house. We heard him pecking away for some time before we found the place where he was working. When we discovered it, we had to undertake a small building repairs operation ourselves. The hen bird repaid us later on by bringing three offspring to the bird-table.

The great spotted woodpecker occasionally comes to the table, and when this happens we all stop work to watch him! The green woodpecker has appeared at

GREEN
WOODPECKER

GREAT
SPOTTED
WOODPECKER

times. A few years ago we saw them more often than the spotted, but I think that they suffered badly in the hard winter of 1962-63. We have certainly not seen so many lately, nor heard the distinctive "yaffle" so frequently. Undoubtedly the wood-pigeons were the birds to suffer most severely in our district that winter, but they have not taken long to re-establish their numbers, much to the chagrin of the farmers.

The robins are a perennial joy to us. There are two that stake out permanent territory round the house, and pretty aggressive they can be. They are completely tame.

At one time there was a particularly enterprising fellow who constantly invaded the kitchen. Finally he grew so bold that he feasted out of the mixing bowl. One day

when my wife discovered four tits and a robin in the kitchen she decided in the interests of hygiene, that a line must be drawn between friendship and licence, so the windows were kept shut for a time.

A variety of warblers come into the garden. I find them practically impossible to differentiate. Unluckily I have absolutely no ear for music, so am unable to recognize them by their songs.

WREN

Sometimes a wren will come to sing his tremendous song for our benefit. I am always astounded that such a very small body can produce such a powerful volume of sound.

Charms of goldfinches frequently appear. Usually we see them in the rough grass feeding on thistle seeds, but at times they come to the inner garden. I think they are almost as fascinating to watch as the flycatchers. It is amazing to think that a small bird can perch on the top of a tall grass without bending it. If the phrase "as light as thistledown" can be applied to anything, it would be to the goldfinch.

A bullfinch will occasionally appear to give us a sight of his lovely plumage. Perhaps it is as well for our orchard that bullfinches are not very prolific in our part of the country, or we might not admire him so unreservedly.

CHAFFINCH

GOLDFINCH

BULLFINCH

Chaffinches, locally known as "pinks" or "pea-finches", are constantly with us, as are the dunnocks. I always think that the rather dull plumage of the dunnock is more than compensated for by the brilliant blue of their eggs.

Our local missel-thrush has several vantage points on which he can sit "blowing up for rain". One is the stone ball on top of the pillar by our gate. He frequently sits there to issue his warning, and it is seldom that we find the "storm-cock" proved to be wrong.

I find it hard to dislike any garden birds, but I must admit that I do not like starlings. I can see little in their favour. They are messy, they occupy nesting sites which

I would prefer to see inhabited by more attractive species, and they take an undue share of the offerings on the bird-table. However, we have them in large numbers. Nor am I very pleased with the jackdaws. They make continual assaults on our chimney pots, even removing the wire protection that we put up with considerable trouble. Fortunately for us, since the Parochial Council repaired the church tower and some ancient elms at the end of the garden have been felled, their numbers are considerably reduced.

April 16th is traditionally the day on which we expect the first cuckoo. Like everybody we are delighted to hear him announce that "Spring is here", and like everybody, we can get bored with him in time. Actually it is some years since his repetitive call went on continuously enough to become a nuisance, but we are well aware that it may happen again. Since I found a cuckoo's egg in a blackcap's nest, I am never sure that I welcome them in the vicinity of the garden.

Mallard are fairly constantly on the pond and the river. They are sometimes very noisy, particularly I think when there are two drakes and one duck present. Being woken in March by a tremendous quacking from the pond, is to me one of the first signs that winter is ending. I fear that they seldom raise a family, in fact it is not often that a brood has been hatched at all. Their natural enemies are too numerous—the pond is full of fair sized pike, and in spite of my efforts to keep them away, there are always carrion crows about. However, the foxes are by far the most serious menace. I have had so much enjoyment out of fox-hunting that I find it hard to deny a fox anything, but I do resent their destruction of our mallard.

Moorhens are permanently with us. On occasion they

have come up over the big lawn to invade our inner garden. Swans are frequent visitors, but they are hardly entitled to be looked upon as wild birds, since I have no doubt that they are the property either of the Queen or the Vintners Company.

KINGFISHER

There is often a kingfisher on the river but we do not see much of him. The sight of one flashing up or down stream is always a notable occasion. Once one sat on a branch as though posed for a photograph for such a long time that it became a question as to which of us would move first. They are not as common as I should like them to be; I wish we had more of them.

NIGHTJAR

We have had occasional visits from night-jars, hearing their distinctive "Coo-ick, Coo-ick" round the house at night. I remember on one occasion being woken up by my daughter, who had not experienced this, to be told in a hoarse whisper—"Daddy, there is someone in the garden calling 'Coo-ee'!"

27

Lapwings are not particularly common in our district, but we do get them in the fields. One July, to our surprise, we saw quite a number in the early mornings and evenings on the lawn within about twenty yards of the house. These visits lasted for about a fortnight. This was undoubtedly, a very strange thing for them to do. I can only think that there was a big hatch of crane fly or some other particularly choice item of their menu which enticed them so close. Other unusual visitors from the fields have been field-fares. A pair of them sat on our garden railing quite close to our window for some time one March day. I think they must have been preparing to migrate. The fact that these two species came, entitles them to be included in our list of birds seen in the garden.

PIED WAGTAIL

TREE CREEPER

LONG-TAILED TIT

Sometimes we have long-tailed tits in the trees round the pond, but we do not see them as often as I would expect. Tree-creepers are with us in fair numbers, but one can feel no surprise at not seeing the little "tree mouse" very often. We have once or twice had grey wagtails by the pond, although they are not regular visitors. The pied wagtails are, but not in the numbers that we had at one time. The fact that a very bushy montana where they used to nest has been taken over by starlings, may I fear account for this.

28

One year when there was a big cross-bill invasion in this country, a party of them visited us. I regret to say that I entirely failed to see them. I could hear them in the tree and the ground beneath it was covered with gnawed husks and cones, but they managed to remain completely invisible. I was not surprised at this as I once spent a month encamped in a Norfolk wood where cross-bills lived in large numbers, and I never caught sight of one of them.

CROSSBILL

Herons pay us fairly frequent visits. As there are only coarse fish in either the pond or the river, I have no objection to their presence. I always feel I have much to learn from their stillness and patience at the waterside.

Perhaps one should not really consider game birds to be garden residents, but one knows of many gardens where pheasants nest regularly. Although there is nearly always a cock bird strutting about on our lawn in winter, we have only once found a nest. On that occasion my wife, while picking daffodils in the rough grass, almost put her hand on a sitting hen. I fear she did not raise her brood. Our resident foxes saw to that.

A more unusual event occurred, when a partridge nested and reared her young behind our greenhouse. That was many years ago. Today in our part of the country, as in many others, the partridge is almost extinct. It is only occasionally that we see them on our walks.

We are quite well supplied with owls. The barn owl sometimes gives us an "exhibition flight" when he carries out a mouse hunt over the rough grass below the lawn. I doubt if any other land bird can give such a magnificent example of controlled gliding. One pair nested in a pollarded elm at the top of the kitchen garden, where the constant hissing of the youngsters was quite annoying to the occupants of the gardener's cottage. The tawny owl is also a resident. Is there anything more pleasant on a frosty night than to fall asleep listening to a distant "Twit-Twoo"?

We have unhappily the usual predators in the form of carrion crows and magpies. They are always about, usually at a safe distance away, but they come right up to the house in the early mornings. I always regret that the magpie is a menace because he is such a very handsome fellow, but I can see nothing whatever in favour of the crow. I wage ceaseless war on them at times when the garden birds are nesting and although they are too cunning for me to do them much damage, I think that my efforts help to keep them at a distance.

Rooks should probably not be included in garden birds, but they are constantly flying over us. The rookery is far enough from the house for the noise not to be obtrusive. We are very glad to have them there, as they have not always been with us. Thirty years ago they were in the long belt that runs along the side of the park. Each year they moved their nests a little farther up the belt. Then, about twenty years ago, they left altogether, a sign I feared that the trees might be getting rotten. However, they returned in small numbers about eight years later building half a dozen nests all in the same tree. A strong gale in March blew the tree down, thus destroying one of my cherished beliefs that rooks never build in a tree that is in any way dangerous. Needless to say, after this episode they were away for a few years. Now they are back, the number of the nests increasing annually, but they have moved the colony to a spinney at the far end of the park. There is an old story that their presence means good fortune to a house, and that if they leave misfortune will follow. An old wives' tale no doubt, but all the same, I hope they will stay.

I have not mentioned all the species of birds that frequent our garden, and whose presence give us such a lot of pleasure. We have listed forty-seven different varieties that have been with us at one time or another. No doubt if we were more knowledgeable in identifying warblers, this number would be higher still. We are indeed fortunate that the surroundings should prove so attractive to birds.

BUSTER

CHAPTER FOUR

Spaniels

S PRINGER spaniels are, in my opinion, about the best "all-round" dogs that anyone could wish for. I have read that they probably conform to the mediaeval spaniel more closely than any other breed, and can be looked upon as its most direct descendant. Certainly they provide all the qualities that most dog owners require. They are good house dogs, highly intelligent, faithful and a useful all-round shooting dog. For a great many years we kept one or more of them. Each had special individual qualities that have left endearing memories. As I get very little covert shooting or grouse driving, I have never needed a high class retriever. For my purposes the series of springers that have shared our home have answered any shooting requirements. In every other respect they have more than fulfilled the role of a dog in the home.

Buster was the first of his kind to come to us. He came

by chance from a friend in South Wales who wished to find a home for him. He had been keeper trained, and had always lived in a kennel. I do not suppose that he had been an object of great interest to anybody. I was the first person on whom he could fix his affection, and as he was the first dog that I had after returning from a spell abroad, we each found in the other what we were looking for.

Nobody could say that Buster was handsome, in spite of his very attractive head. I think that he had a cross of Clumber in his ancestry, being decidedly heavier in front than behind, with legs that might be described as slightly knock-kneed. His movements were apt to be ungainly, but his activity seemed unimpaired. On one occasion when he had succeeded in retrieving a grouse that my host's labrador had failed to find, the keeper exclaimed— "Ah, the little rickety dog has it!"

A remark that did not please me at all, although, it sent my fellow guests, with whom incidentally, Buster was a great favourite, into peels of unseemly laughter.

At the time that Buster came to me I was an instructor at the Royal Military College. He dropped into the routine of my work very easily. I do not think that he ever missed a lecture, sitting sedately under my desk throughout the period. He showed admirable restraint in resisting all surreptitious attempts by cadets to lure him out with pieces of biscuit, or by other means to attract his attention.

As might be expected almost every officer in the College owned a dog. Buster was on good terms with most of them. There was only one which he, in company with every dog on the place, looked upon as a deadly enemy; this was a big long-legged cross-bred springer, belonging to the Commandant. Without being in any

B

way savage, this dog was an inveterate bully, so that other dog owners always gave him a wide berth. I well remember one unfortunate fracas in which he and Buster were involved.

For some reason the Commandant had summoned me to the "Top Office". Thinking that the Commandant's dog would certainly be in the office with his master, I allowed Buster to come with me, as he of course would remain outside while I went in for my interview. My consternation can well be imagined, when as we mounted the stairs, I saw the dog sitting on the landing.

When one considers the number of times that Buster must have heard me lecture on tactics, it is regrettable that he "appreciated the situation" so badly. Instead of realising at once that he was faced by a force of over-whelming strength in a confined space, and making use of such mobility as he possessed to get down the stairs and out on to the square, he cowered on a half-landing. Here his opponent put in an all out attack.

The ensuing battle, although not serious from the point of view of damage to either antagonist, was ex-tremely noisy. Office doors flew open all round the landing. The Adjutant and the Battalion Sergeant-Major were so aghast at the sacrilege committed in the sacred precincts of "Top Office", that their advice was of negligible value. The Commandant, who appeared in person, was so convulsed with laughter that he was unable even to call off his own dog. In the end the con-testants were separated by a couple of cadets who were on the landing, waiting I think, adjudication on some misdemeanour.

One of my fellow instructors with whom I spent a good deal of time owned a black cocker spaniel who rejoiced in the name of Chumpy. Buster and Chumpy were great friends. We frequently took them riding with us on the heath land behind the College. I have pleasant memories of canters down "the Ladies Mile" which always ended in a wait at "Lower Star Post" until two panting spaniels had caught up with us. Oddly enough, Chumpy who was quite happy to come if Buster was there, thoroughly objected to going on his own. If his master took him for a lone ride he would take the first opportunity to sneak off home.

Another happy recollection is an occasion at the end of the summer term, when my friend and I organized a rather light hearted "chart and compass" race for our class. It ended at the bathing lake where everyone went in for a swim. Neither Buster nor Chumpy liked the idea of the water. They stood together at the end of the diving board whimpering unhappily while their masters splashed about below them. In the end they could not stand it any longer, so with a couple of heavy splashes they joined us in the water.

I had Buster for about nine years. When he died there was a variety of dogs in the house belonging to different members of the family. Before I had acquired a personal dog to replace him, World War II had broken out.

The first thing that I did after the war ended was to set about acquiring a spaniel. The result of my efforts was Sally. She came from a breeder by whom she had been gun-trained, so that house training was all that was required when she arrived with us. Considering that Sally was no longer a puppy she picked this up very easily, the only thing that she was slow to take to was her basket. At first she looked upon this with deep suspicion, but once she had appreciated its purpose, she loved it. Sally was well bred and a very pretty dog, in fact far the best looking of any of our spaniels. She was just over a

35

year old when she came, and I had her for ten years.

I benefited by Sally's arrival in more ways than one. Not only had I a personal dog (my children already had a Pekinese and an Aberdeen terrier in the house) but she was incidental in getting me quite a bit of extra shooting. I was one of the earliest of my neighbours to get a spaniel, so for a season or two, a gun who could bring a dog with him was doubly welcome.

SALLY.

Sally was good at her job, hunting out well and retrieving excellently. Her only fault was that nothing would stop her running-in. She had the flattering, but entirely erroneous idea, that every time her master fired, there would inevitably be something to pick up! However, for the usual type of shooting I got, this did not do much harm. If we took part in a covert shoot I kept her tied down.

There was one occasion when she gave me cause to blush. I was shooting with a friend, who although the best of good fellows, was apt to get irascible if things did not go according to plan. We were having a day "pottering", and were going through a series of small spinneys. While moving from one to another, a pheasant got up at my feet. Shot or no shot, this was too much for Sally, who immediately rushed off in pursuit. The pheasant pitched in the covert that we were approaching, and despite all my whistling, Sally followed it in. It was only a small place, so that in no time birds were bursting out in all directions. I glanced round at my host in time to see him stamping on his hat! I did not dare go to apologize. Luckily Sally realized fairly quickly that she had committed a grave breach of decorum, and returned with a somewhat shame faced expression.

Probably in her old age, the happiest shooting memories that Sally might have looked back on, would have been a week that we spent walking grouse in Inverness-shire. There were only three guns, a lot of birds, and we went out every day. The only other dog belonged to the keeper, a not very efficient Labrador. Sally had almost all the work to do, receiving a great deal of praise from everyone. I know nothing more pleasant than seeing one's dog giving universal satisfaction to a shooting party. How much ground she covered I do not like to think. By the end of the fifth day even she had had enough. While I was dressing on Saturday morning she lay quite quiet without showing any excitement. As I left the room she gave me a look that said quite plainly—

"Master, I am not coming today."

So for the first and only time, I left her behind. I think that she probably slept all day.

When Sally had been with me for two or three years I decided to breed from her. I chose for a sire a springer belonging to a neighbour of mine. I later discovered that this was not a very satisfactory choice, as the dog although a good worker, was highly strung, a disability that he passed on to his progeny. Sally produced a litter of nine, but on the advice of the vet. this number was reduced to five, as in his opinion she would not be able to rear more. We kept one puppy for ourselves, to be the personal property of my wife, and called her Jane. Sally was an excellent mother, as in later years, she was to prove a very good foster-mother.

Jane was very much her father's daughter. Like him she was a big dog in every way, like him unfortunately, she was highly strung. As she grew older she became subject to attacks of hysteria if anything caused her great excitement. She inherited little of Sally's beauty, but she had considerable attraction. Nobody could pretend that she was intelligent, in point of fact she was a fool, but a very lovable fool.

While she was a puppy, she decided that the best place to occupy in the car was the ledge under the rear window. This was a perfectly satisfactory position while she was small, but as she grew up, it became extremely cramped. By the time that she was full grown she had to lie with her legs hanging down, a position that looked extremely uncomfortable. However, nothing would induce her to sit anywhere else.

On one occasion when we thought that she was a bit short of exercise, we let her out of the car to run behind us for about half a mile up our drive. She thought this was tremendous fun, stretching out in the field alongside us like a greyhound. From that day onwards she insisted on being allowed to do this. As soon as the car turned into the drive gate, she would be off her window seat whimpering with anticipation until we let her out of the car. One great advantage of her long legs was that she was an excellent dog to take out riding with us. In fact she enjoyed some of our longer rides more than Sally did.

We trained Jane to the gun at home, but we did not take her shooting very often, and then only if my wife was coming too. The excitement was apt to prove too much for her, bringing on a hysterical attack. Curiously enough if I went alone with Sally, she never fretted or worried about being left. I think that it was quite clear in her mind that if my wife stayed at home, she stayed too.

While she was still a puppy, Jane acquired a Teddy bear which she found on my daughter's bed. Not relishing the idea of tucking up with a much mouthed toy, my daughter made her a present of it. From that moment Jane never left it far away when she was in the house. A day came when Teddy could not be found. No doubt it had been taken out of doors and left somewhere. Jane was quite miserable, in fact so unhappy did she appear, that a friend who was staying with us, presented her with another one. She seemed to derive some extraordinary comfort from it. If she showed signs of getting overwrought, the quickest way to steady her down was to throw Teddy to her. If anything excited her, such as the arrival of a number of people in the house, she would at once seize her toy and run round with it. I think that this was a comic characteristic that was all her own. I have certainly never heard of any other spaniel behaving in this way.

Jane died when she was about five years old. Not long afterwards my daughter married, taking away her Aberdeen terrier, so we were left with Sally as the only dog in the house.

We at once decided that we must get another spaniel both to be a personal dog for my wife, and a companion for Sally.

Before we had made any enquiries, an unexpected notice appeared in the local paper advertising a litter of springers for which the owner wanted a quick sale. We decided to go to inspect them.

On arrival at the house the reason for a quick sale became obvious. In view of the cold weather the owner had decided to let the puppies sleep in the warmth of his greenhouse. That night a riot had taken place, in the course of which one hundred and thirty-six chrysanthemums had been completely destroyed. When we arrived the puppies were housed in the pig-sty. They were paraded for our inspection.

It was an attractive litter, but it did not take us long to make our selection. One little bitch appeared carrying something in her mouth in a very gentle manner. She had also a highly intelligent look, so we chose her at once. Thus Sue joined our household.

Subsequently we were to question whether we had been wise to be swayed by that look of intelligence. It was undoubtedly there, in fact Sue was by far the most intelligent of our spaniels. She was also the most mischievous and the most difficult to train. If one puppy in that litter was the ringleader in the greenhouse destruction, I am ready to bet that it was Sue. In spite of her devilry, by the time that she grew up, she repaid us amply for the trouble that she had caused in her youth.

The journey home, was of course Sue's first experience of car travel. Not unnaturally she was sick, but, except for one unfortunate occasion at a later date after she had devoured about a pound of butter without our knowledge, it was the only time that this happened. What did amuse us, was Sally's behaviour during the drive. She sat on the back seat resting her chin on my shoulder the whole time. One could almost hear her saying—"You won't take any notice of this thing, will you, master?"

However, when we arrived home Sally realised at once that Sue was my wife's dog, and had nothing at all to do with me. Satisfied on this point, she became a first-class foster-mother, allowing her ears and tail to be pulled without protest. She would even allow Sue to push her aside from the water bowl when she was drinking, but there was one thing at which she drew the line.

S U E.

She would allow no interference with her meals, the least attempt by Sue even to inspect her dinner plate called forth a warning growl. Sally had a peaceful disposition, even for a spaniel. The only time that I ever saw her roused was in defence of Sue. A very ill-tempered terrier living in the village made a menacing advance on the puppy, Sally with a rather ineffective attempt to raise her hackles, hurled herself at the assailant, knocked him down and stood over him uttering furious snarls. After this episode the terrier never came near us.

As has been said, Sue proved very difficult to train.

This was not because she did not know what was required of her, but because she knew only too well and her innate devilry prompted her to do the opposite. We were quite convinced, that not only did she understand every word that we said, but also, in course of time, she understood French and words spelt out as well.

In our dining room each dog has always had its particular place in which to sit. Sue quickly learnt where she was meant to be, but she had not the least intention of conforming. We could see her eyeing us, waiting for an appropriate moment to dash across the room in order to have the satisfaction of being dragged back again. During these performances Sally would sit primly in her corner with a smug expression on her face. A moment came when we thought that we could no longer cope with Sue, and that we should have to get rid of her. We told her so in no uncertain tones. The effect was immediate, she never moved again. The same thing occurred over her basket. She completely destroyed the first one that we gave her. We produced another and she at once started on that. We assured her that if this one was wrecked she would have to do without a basket at all. From that moment she never savaged it again.

It is of course, natural for a puppy to chew up anything that it can get hold of, but Sue and I fell out seriously over the question of the morning papers. It was the custom of the delivery man to leave them on the mat inside the door. Sue would hear him arrive, and immediately dash down stairs to indulge in an orgy of destruction. For some reason the "Times" seemed to be the great attraction, and when I came down, I would be greeted with a wicked look which seemed to say—"I've finished the crossword!" Fortunately, by not allowing her out of the bedroom until we came down ourselves, this propensity was checked.

Sue was very easy to house train and quickly learnt to ask when she wanted to go out. For some time she would wake my wife up night after night and demand to be taken in the garden. My wife noticed that a good deal of the time outdoors was spent in playing with fallen leaves. Finally we decided to take a chance, so the next time it happened she was merely sworn at. All was well and she never asked again.

As Sue grew up her relationship with Sally took on a definite character. There was no doubt that they were very good friends, but Sally quite firmly adopted the position of the "old soldier", while Sue became the respectful and obedient "recruit". It was quite obvious that Sally gave the orders while Sue jumped to the word of command. Sally insisted that she must take the leading part in any operations which were undertaken. When I took Sue out on to the lawn with a gun and blank cartridges to give her first lesson in sitting to shot, I took Sally too, thinking that it would do her no harm to join in the lesson. Nothing could have been less in accordance with Sally's ideas. Once she had heard one or two shots, she realised that the sound was nothing like that of a full charge, so turning a contemptuous back, she returned to the house.

One of Sally's favourite pastimes was to dig for nests of field mice in the rough grass at the bottom of the lawn. I do not think she ever succeeded in getting at one, but nothing damped her ardour. As Sue grew up she was introduced to this form of amusement, and the procedure underwent a change. The pair would go down to the area of search where Sally would choose the spot and start the excavation. Sue immediately joined in the work, so in a very short time Sally would withdraw leaving it all to Sue. It was comic to see Sally sitting up like a martinet, saying quite clearly—"Dig here," while Sue, with all the exuberance of youth, would tear wildly at the ground with teeth and claws. I have seen her on a hot day return to the house gasping for a drink of water, but having had it, she returned at once to her arduous task. During this interlude Sally would remain calmly seated by the hole without attempting to do a stroke of work in the absence of her underling. As soon as she considered the excavation had gone deep enough to be getting near the nest, she would push Sue aside and take over.

When Sally and I had been out shooting, the procedure on our return home was always the same. Sally would sit in front of the fire to dry herself out thoroughly. It was obvious that she was turning the events of the day over in her mind. During this time Sue, apparently entirely on her own initiative, would move round her pulling the burrs out of her coat. I thoroughly approved of this practice as it saved me a lot of trouble with a comb later.

Sally died at the age of eleven. Sue missed her very much, fretting quite badly for several days. However, she settled down as the only dog in the house, naturally becoming very much the centre of things. I did not get a lot of shooting, so she was quite adequate for my requirements in this respect.

Sue had all her shooting training at home, which was not really very satisfactory. Had she been trained by an expert and worked with a keeper, I have little doubt that she would have proved a very high class dog. She had a good mouth, and a really excellent nose, but she was wild and headstrong. We were never able to give her enough work to keep her steady. Sometimes she was a source of of pride to us, at other times quite definitely the opposite.

One of the first occasions on which we took her out was to walk with the guns through an extremely thick, bramble infested wood. Our host, a very imperious elderly sportsman, was no longer able to shoot himself, but he stumped down the rides making sure that his guns were carrying out his instructions. Early on in the day he ordered one man to take his dog back to his car on account of its riotous behaviour. He came upon my wife with Sue on a lead hoping for an opportunity to send her in to pick up.

"Why don't you let your dog go?" he asked.

"Well," said my wife, "She is only young and she might be wild."

"A spaniel is no good if it does not hunt. Let her go," the old man ordered peremptorily.

In deep trepidation my wife let her loose. Luckily for all concerned the covert was so thick that even Sue was daunted; she behaved impeccably all day.

Very often my wife and Sue used to go with the beaters. This was a job that suited Sue down to the ground, as she could be fairly wild without doing any damage, and she was expert at getting birds out of thick places. One day she came out of covert at the end of a drive in hot pursuit of a low flying cock-pheasant, which she continued to chase across the field. More as a gesture than with any hope of success my wife blew her whistle. To our complete surprise, Sue stopped at once and came straight in.—"What an obedient dog," remarked one of the guns who had just appeared upon the scene.

There were times however, when she completely "blotted her copy book". One particular incident that caused us acute embarrassment, occurred when we were out with quite a large party after snipe in the area of the local sewage farm. Shooting was over and we were on our

way back to our cars. Suddenly, for no apparent reason, Sue made a dash into an enormous, extremely boggy patch of reeds. We could see by the movement of the rushes where she was dashing madly about, but whistling for her had no effect whatever. Suddenly pheasants began to appear. I was appalled as I knew that our host would not want them disturbed. He looked upon this patch of reeds as a kind of covert which could be beaten out before having a walk round the neighbouring hedgerows. Certainly he would not wish to see everything put out of it at the end of a day. For about twenty minutes Sue pursued her activities under the gaze of the assembled guns who were waiting to go home. When she was certain that nothing remained to chase, she returned completely covered with stinking black mud. My host on that day has not asked me to shoot again!

Sue thoroughly enjoyed going into water. There was nothing that she liked better than retrieving a duck that had fallen in the pond. She was also quite insane about moorhens. I have been told by a keeper that the scent of these birds is known to be very strong, and she thought them even more thrilling than partridges. Twice in her life Sue gave us severe frights. The second occasion was in her old age when a covey of partridges nearly proved the end of her. While we were out for a walk the birds got up at our feet causing her to race off in such wild excitement that she was completely exhausted. I had to carry her home, and for the future, we restricted our walks with her to the home grounds. But the first of the incidents to make us thoroughly scared was caused by a moorhen.

We were at the Charlton ponds where we had gone to inspect the sluice and the silt trap after particularly heavy rain. A moorhen got up with much noise and flew across the main pond. Sue immediately went in after it, getting across without any difficulty as it was fairly narrow and clear of weed at that place. The bird in the meantime moved up the bank to the broadest part where it flew back again. At this place the whole centre of the pond was a thick weed bed. Sue was after it again in a flash. I was certain that she would get hung up, so I hurried off to get the boat. However, without the least hesitation, she went straight into the weed bed, pushed her way through with a considerable struggle and landed safely on the other side. Here my wife promptly put a lead on her before any further aquatic performances could be indulged in.

Sue has left us with many amusing memories. She was an adept at catching moths once they flew low enough to be within her reach. As my wife has a distinct aversion to all insects, this ability was made full use of, particularly in our bedroom. She knew precisely at what hour we got up in the morning, so if we were still asleep at that time she would wake my wife. Sue's method of doing this was to put a large paw on her face, which was apt to be painful. In the end I had to put up a barricade formed by the early morning tea trolley to keep her at a distance. Even then, no alarm clock was needed as she whimpered until she saw us make a move.

One final incident comes to my mind. A friend came round to see us (incidentally he had been the owner of Chumpy in the distant days at Sandhurst) at a moment when I was up a ladder painting the garage doors, with Sue sitting peacefully below me. Calling to me that he had only come for a moment to consult my wife on some point, he went into the house leaving his car door open. On his return he found that some bacon and plaice that were the outcome of a morning's shopping had gone. Sue was back sitting complacently at the foot of my ladder. My friend took his loss in good part, but he was rather riled when the only remark that the fishmonger made when he went to buy another piece of plaice was—

"My goodness, wasn't it lucky that the fish was filleted!"

Sue died at the ripe age of fourteen. She had been a delightful companion and we missed her terribly. We decided not to have another springer. The amount of shooting that I get now does not warrant a dog specifically for that purpose. Furthermore, with increasing years we did not feel like going through the business of training another, and giving it the amount of exercise a young dog would need. In fact we have not up to the present, replaced her with any dog at all. We frequently ponder Kipling's lines—

"Brothers and Sisters, I bid you beware
Of giving your heart to a dog to tear."

Nevertheless, I think there will be another occupant for the basket in time.

CHAPTER FIVE

Characters

I HAVE been extremely fortunate for many years in the men whom I have had in my employ. There are three in particular I always think of with gratitude.

Yates was my gardener for about twenty years. He was a local man, born and brought up in the village. His first job as a boy, was leading the horse that drew the heavy roller over the lawn in front of my house. Except for the period of the First World War when he served in France with the R.G.A., and a short spell as far away as Birmingham, the whole of his working life was spent in North Buckinghamshire.

In our part of the country we make considerable use of the adjective "awkward". Local pronunciation turns this into "okkard" and it is the perfect description of a mood which besets most of us at times. Yates was more or less permanently "okkard". Nothing ever seemed to go the way he wanted, so that life was inclined to become a continual grouse. Once this was understood, and the necessary allowance made, Yates was a first-class man to work with.

He was of a taciturn disposition, more inclined to show his disapprobation by his manner than in words. This led us into difficulties at times. On many occasions my wife and I have come upon him looking disconsolately into the middle of a flower bed or a vegetable plot. As one approached, an arm with a pointing finger would be extended, and a grim voice would say—"Look at that". Since we were seldom able to see at first glance what it was that was causing his disapproval, we found that the best course was to reply in a sympathetic voice—"Oh, Yates". Having thus registered that one was just as unhappy about everything as he was, the cause of the grievance would be disclosed.

I remember one incident which gave Yates a very justifiable cause for a grouse. A flock of hawfinches descended early one morning on his green peas, which were just ready for picking. It took them no time at all to strip the lot. I have never seen anyone more upset, nor, on this occasion, was my own commiseration with him in any way insincere. In fact I had two causes of complaint over the episode. Not only had I lost the first picking of peas, but I myself had not seen the hawfinches. They are not often with us, and I do not think that they have been here since. So I missed the sight of an uncommon visitor.

The activities of children in the garden are never regarded with much indulgence by the gardener. Yates and my children seldom saw eye to eye. Jumping competitions over flower-beds or shrubs were not, in his opinion, amusements to be encouraged, nor did the practice of indiscriminate fruit and flower picking commend itself to him. All the same he was very capable of holding his own, so that the children went in considerable awe of him. On the other hand he was no sneak, and I think they realised this. He did not as a rule come to me with complaints about them; in fact only once can I remember him doing so. On that occasion he was so incensed with my younger daughter, that he forgot her name, and referred to her by the name of a lady who had been a child in one of his earlier places. Clearly the "Gardener v Children" War had a long history behind it.

Like most gardeners Yates had a strong aversion to picking his peas and beans or digging his potatoes when they were really young. In my opinion this is the only time that vegetables are really fit to eat, so this point formed a permanent bone of contention between us. A request for early peas would produce an attack of "okkardness" almost beyond belief. It was not every time that I could get my way in this matter, but when I did, one might have thought from the resultant gloom that the hawfinches were with us again!

Although undoubtedly a difficult character, Yates was a first class gardener. When I appealed to him for advice he would always end up his instructions with the words—"if you don't mind my telling you". Naturally one was only too glad to be told, as his knowledge of gardening was profound. He was also a skilled carpenter. There are several small things in my house which he made for me, from the wood of uncommon trees which had been felled on the place. He took a leading part in all village affairs, sitting on the Parish Council, singing in the Choir, and in his younger days, playing in the cricket team.

Yates died within a few days of the death of his wife. She had also lived in the village since she had been a girl, so they left quite a gap in the community. Yates was a character such as one seldom meets today, and I think that the countryside is the poorer for it.

*   *   *

After Yates' death I gave considerable thought to the question of his successor. Yates had been a gardener pure and simple, claiming no knowledge of machinery or any work outside the garden. During the two last years of his life, when he had been a sick man, much of the garden had unfortunately been neglected. It was obvious that in the future the whole place would have to be re-organized on a more labour saving basis. The garden area would have to be reduced, giving time to cope with other commitments. I therefore advertised for a "gardener-handyman". Hartwell, who came in reply to this, proved to be exactly what I required.

At our interview Hartwell told me that he had worked on a farm, and was capable of any field work that I might require. He had looked after a garden, and that gardening was work that he really liked; he also said that he was a "rough" carpenter. On all these points he made an understatement. I have not yet found a job which he cannot do, and do well. One has only to put a problem to him, give him twenty-four hours to think it over, and he will produce the solution.

During the twelve years that we have worked together we have made considerable changes. Nearly the whole of the kitchen garden has been converted to an orchard of dwarf apple trees. Many of the flower borders have been taken out altogether, and some of the remaining ones have been changed to rose beds. All the tucked away corners about the place have been tidied up and cleared of old shrubs. It is now much easier to look after, so that in spite of the fact that we are both getting older, we can keep it under control.

On my small acreage of land he has cut-and-laid the hedges, repaired the posts and rails, re-hung the gates and cleaned through the spinneys. Some of our happiest working days have been spent on these jobs. Cutting-and-laying is one of his chief delights, and the more intractable the hedge the better pleased he will be. A rough over-grown stretch that requires planning in advance, and skill in operation is a joy to him. He has given me many lessons in the art, and although I can only take on the easiest parts of a hedge, I have learnt enough to share his enthusiasm.

Like Yates, Hartwell is a local man, only he comes from the other side of "our river"—Northamptonshire. He was born in the county, and except for his time in the Army has spent the whole of his working life in this area. Hartwell was a regular soldier joining the R.A.S.C. prior to the First World War and serving until the end of it. After his discharge he started working on the land, thereafter remaining in that form of employment.

54

How Hartwell acquired his wide variety of accomplishments I do not know. He maintains that his father could turn his hand to anything, and that as soon as he himself was old enough to help him, made sure that his son should be able to do the same. The fact remains that from cobbling to drystone walling, from draining to making furniture, nothing comes amiss to him. His gardening is to some extent self-taught, gardening magazines being his favourite form of reading, but on this subject also his knowledge is extensive. On all matters of general interest his comments are shrewd and very much to the point.

Hartwell has many outstanding characteristics, but one which gives us both a great deal of amusement is what I call his "white knight" complex. He will never throw anything away, maintaining that "it might come in useful some day". The curious thing is that it nearly always does come in useful. Time and again when there has been some little job to be done he has said to me—

"I think I can find just the thing for that." The thing may in fact, take quite a lot of finding, because he has very likely forgotten where he put it, but sooner or later, it comes to light, and sure enough, it fulfils the purpose for which it was wanted.

An aspect of gardening of which Hartwell had no experience before coming to me was lawn mowing on a large scale. I have a considerable area of grass which needs to be cut regularly. It took him no time at all to master the big mower, both on the mechanical side and in operation. Now our weekly mowing day is one that he probably enjoys more than any other. It is diverting to watch him seated on the roller attachment, swinging the big machine round like a polo-pony, to bring it accurately down the long level lines of the cut. He makes it

55

look extremely easy, but I know in fact, that it calls for a great deal of skill. I tell him that he would be perfectly capable of driving the machine in a bending race.

One of Hartwell's most successful enterprises is growing tomatoes. In our unheated greenhouse he produces them in great quantities, endeavouring each season to beat the total of the weight grown in the previous year. When they are over, the chrysanthemums are brought in to benefit from the well composted soil in which the tomatoes had been grown. When tried for the first time as an experiment this proved an immediate success. As a result my wife always has some lovely blooms for the house and plenty of flowers for the Church at Christmas time.

Hartwell also made a pedestal for displaying the flowers in church. He gave it an ingenious top of his own design, which enables them to be arranged to perfection.

I think that one reason for Hartwell's all round efficiency is the extremely methodical way in which he organises his work. He keeps a detailed diary of jobs done each day, so that it is always available to show which seasonal tasks are falling due. He also keeps a list of non-regular items that are outstanding, particularly those that can be carried out in bad weather. Consequently the day which we sometimes refer to as "when we have nothing else to do", has never yet arrived! The only time that I have seen his programme upset was in the winter of 1962/63 when for nine long weeks we were under deep snow. During that period, once the routine chores of keeping the approaches open, and getting water to the house were finished (for 32° of frost had frozen up our pipes underground), we really did find ourselves at a loose end. We neither of us enjoyed that time, but I think that Hartwell hated it more than I did.

Needless to say Hartwell has a "way" with animals. In the past he has had a good deal of shepherding experience, including the handling and training of sheep dogs. Our spaniel Sue loved him, and in his opinion she could do no wrong. If we went away, leaving her at home, reports of her behaviour during our absence were always completely without criticism.

One of Hartwell's idiosyncracies is the possession of an enormous assortment of coats and hats. These are left in every shed round the place, so as to be immediately available whenever required. It is a standing joke between us, that I judge the weather conditions, entirely by the type of clothing that he is wearing when he passes our windows in the morning, and I equip myself accordingly.

I have said that Hartwell's reading is almost entirely books on gardening, but he is also a television fan and an addict to Scrabble. I myself do not particularly care for television, but we find ourselves welcome visitors to Hartwell's cottage for the Grand National. This is a standing invitation, and we have enjoyed watching the race together for many years. At Scrabble he is the acknowledged master in his household. I understand that at odd times he spends a few minutes looking up words in the dictionary, so as to have some ready to deal with difficult letters. This is just another example of the care and method which he applies to everything.

Hartwell has a great sense of humour which adds to the pleasure of working with him. I hope that we may continue together for many years to come.

*　　　*　　　*

It was a very lucky day for me when Taylor answered my advertisement for a groom. I was at that time still a serving officer, but the fact that he would be continually on the move did not worry him in the least. He remained with me until his death about twenty years later.

While I was in the Service, Taylor had not only to move with me from station to station, but also to take hunters to different places for my leave in winter, and polo ponies to tournaments all over the country in summer. It did not matter to him where he went as long as he was with his horses—he asked nothing more.

On my retirement from the army, Taylor became my stud-groom with very considerable responsibilities. Not only did I myself keep a fair number of hunters and children's ponies, but most seasons a brother officer would stay for his winter leave bringing a couple of horses and a soldier groom. These also were placed under Taylor's charge. In addition to the horses, there were always two couple of hound puppies at walk with us, for whose upbringing he was entirely responsible. During the years that the stables were under his control I never had cause for one moments anxiety.

Some people have an in-born sympathy with horses—Taylor was one. Whether he was working or not, he was constantly with his charges. He never stopped talking to them. When he was going round the yard the unceasing conversation might have led one to believe that there were two people present. I was told that every night he looked out of his bedroom window to say good-night to them. On the occasions when we went to polo tournaments he would never let me take lodgings for him. He preferred to put up a bed in the saddle room, in case the ponies should feel lonely in a strange stable. It goes without saying that he could do anything with them. In summer when he walked round to "look-over" the horses at grass, he had no difficulty in approaching them. In fact one would see a little group in the middle of the field, each one waiting its turn to be petted and inspected. Nor was it only with animals that he knew well that Taylor could make immediate contact. One season I was lent a hunter that belonged to a neighbour, who was very experienced and sympathetic with horses. She told me she had never been able to clip it out round the head, so that I would have to put up with the indignity of hunting a horse with a shaggy face. I agreed to put up with that, but before the horse had been in my stable a week, its head was clipped as neatly as the rest of its body.

Taylor was a first class horse master. I doubt if I ever had a horse out of work due to coughs, colds or digestive troubles. He had served during the First World War with the R.A.V.C. and had clearly taken full advantage of

59

that experience. Except for major accidents I never called on the services of a vet during the whole time that he was with me.

When I consider the standard of smartness that Taylor demanded from everything concerned with the horses and stables, I cannot help smiling at my recollection of his own turnout. He was one of those people who just could not be smart. A new suit, when he had worn it for a month, seemed to lose all shape, and his efforts at tying a hunting tie achieved deplorable results. This however was his only failing.

There were usually one or two grey horses in my stables. These Taylor always groomed himself, as he maintained that none of his stablemen could turn out a grey properly. I always suspected that he must have used "Reckitts blue" or some such concoction during the process. When the horses were sent on to a meet, I would find them tucked away in a corner with Taylor giving everything a last "go over" with a rubber. The final act, before the cloth disappeared into his tail pocket, was to give my boots a rub over after I had mounted!

The same principle was applied in the stable yard where tidiness was insisted upon. I remember hearing my small son severely told off for coming out of a box dragging straw on his feet. He was firmly ordered to pick it all up and put it back in the box. Possibly Taylor's proudest moments were on Sunday mornings. He knew that I would visit the stables to discuss arrangements for the week following. He also knew that anybody staying with us would certainly come to have a look at the horses. He was determined that everything should be immaculate. Stable buckets with my initials neatly painted on them had to be outside each box; all the horses were in Sunday rugs and head-collars, the latter with newly blancoed white brow bands; carrots were laid out in the saddle room, washed and sliced ready for distribution, while a long stable coat covered any possible defects in his own attire. As the majority of my guests were hunting men who had known Taylor for many years, the gossip and banter that took place was a joy to his heart.

Mention of the carrots reminds me that Taylor grew his own for the stables. He was always prepared to turn his hand to anything that would benefit his beloved horses. He was no gardener, but as he and Yates failed to see eye to eye on the subject of carrots for the stables out of the kitchen garden, he decided to dig a bit of ground and put some seed in for himself. Like many rather amateur enterprises this turned out trumps. Sometimes we were inclined to think that the carrots which we saw in the stables were better than the ones that we saw in the house!

Taylor and my children were the firmest friends. He took them each in turn on a leading rein, both hacking and hunting until they were experienced enough to go on their own. It is a great regret to me that he did not live long enough to see my son have his first win in a point-to-point. Taylor was very firm with them, standing no nonsense. Everything both in stables and out riding, had to be done in the correct manner. They never thought of disobeying his orders. I was most amused on one occasion, to hear him reprove my son for saying— "Damn you"—to one of his sisters. "I will have no swearing in my stables," was the order. When I considered, that whatever his standard might be in stables, Taylor had a fine flow of language outside them, I thought that there was something in the saying about Satan rebuking sin!

An amusing incident involving Taylor comes to my mind. I subscribe to the old superstition that one should take off ones hat and say "Good morning" to a magpie. On one occasion when we were riding on to a meet together, a magpie crossed in front of us, so I duly took off my hat. Seeing this, Taylor concluded that an acquaintance was approaching and doffed his as well. Nothing was said to me at the time, but his wife told us afterwards that when he reported the incident to her he ended by saying,—"And when I looked round I found that I had taken my hat off to a b----y bird!"

With the outbreak of the Second World War my hunter stables were naturally closed down. One horse for me to ride when I came on leave, and the children's ponies were kept available either at grass or roughed up in stable. Taylor turned his hand to anything that could in any way help the family. Some cows were purchased of which he took charge, doing the milking and rearing the calves. The kennels for the hound puppies became a chicken run also under his supervision. At haymaking time he organized everything and built the rick himself.

Among the many ways in which Taylor helped the household, was an attempt to relieve the transport difficulties caused by the laying up of the car. An ancient wagonette was procured and my hunter was harnessed to it for undertaking local journeys. The mare did not take at all kindly to the experiment. My wife has vivid recollections of being met at the station by Taylor with this equippage. She was bidden to get into the vehicle and hold the reins while Taylor stood at the mare's head. As soon as he let go, off the mare went while Taylor raced round, took a flying leap on to the box seat, and seized the reins. Once on board he took control, and the party returned home at a hand gallop! A most unnerving experience.

While I was abroad I had one or two personal letters from Taylor. I appreciated these very much, as I knew that writing was not his strong point, and that nothing but real friendship would have inspired them.

During the last year of the war he became a sick man, and by the time that I got home he was no longer fit for active work. I got the stables going again with the help of my children, Taylor being in the background to advise. In a few months one of the men who had been under him before the war was demobilized, and returned to take over the care of the horses. From then on the stables were operating in a small way, but to me they were never the same. The difficulties of hunting have obviously increased in recent years, but I feel, had Taylor lived to be in charge of my limited stud, I should still be hunting today.

Taylor was still a comparatively young man when he died. My family owe him an enormous debt of gratitude. He was linked with some of the happiest times that we all had together. I like to think that they were happy days for him too.

I have learnt much from these three men. It has been a privilege to have been served by, and to have worked

63

with them. When the qualities of efficiency, loyalty, and honesty are combined, no man can ask for more.

CHAPTER SIX

An Annual Cricket Match

THE annual cricket match between the village and a
side from my house, had its origin in the days when I
was still a serving officer. For the first of these games
I brought over a team from my Regiment. On this,
as I think on all subsequent occasions, we were defeated.

The most notable incidents in that first match concerned two of my players. One was my trumpeter, a gay
young fellow who answered to the knickname of
Smacker. He was no great cricketer, although he could
bowl. I think that he had been included in the side on
account of his cheerful disposition. His drawback was
that he had a considerable flow of bad language which
he found hard to control. When bowling, it was his custom to accompany each delivery with loud and profane
comments. His efforts to curb this propensity while the
rector was batting, caused considerable amusement to the

surrounding fieldsmen.

There was only one member of my team who could have been described as a serious cricketer. He was my Quarter-Master Sergeant, a formidable left arm swing bowler, who had more than once played for the army. I did not put him on to bowl at the commencement of our opponents innings, as I thought he might be rather overpowering for a village side. When he did go on, each batsman in turn treated him with contempt to start with, scoring freely off the first two or three balls; but each in turn fell a victim to the curl of the ball in the air. Needless to say he dismissed the opposition, but at a cost which although it might have been of little importance in high class cricket, constituted a considerable score by village standards.

After I retired from the army the House v Village match became a regular fixture. At that time there were a number of men employed in the stables and gardens, some of whom could play cricket, all of whom were prepared to try. I had an arrangement with the village captain whereby any of his regular players who were in my employ, were entitled to play for the house team. The remainder were recruited from neighbours and guests. The same description could be applied to them as to the employees, except that the proportion who really could play cricket was probably lower. Proficiency on the field was not by any means the main reason for selection.

The sequence of events never varied very much. In the morning the house side usually put in some practice on the lawn, a spectacle which never inspired me with much confidence as to the outcome of the match. The game always started a bit late, the village enjoying the relaxation from the strict timings of their league matches.

Tea was served in the Village Hall, without any tiresome nonsense about a limited period for its consumption. Should a second innings be possible, this was played on a time basis, and both teams reversed their batting order. The house side went further by making a rule that every-one should bowl two overs. Curiously enough, our score in these circumstances was usually rather better than in the first innings, but the bowling rule got us into some diffi-culties. I remember one of my friends making a delivery that came out behind him, narrowly missing the umpire. In his case, a considerable time elapsed before two overs of balls within reach of the batsman were completed.

There were many comic incidents in the matches played during the years before the war. Once I heard the opposing captain tell his bowler to give me an easy one for the first ball of my innings. This gesture was much appreciated! The games were played in a light-hearted manner, but in spite of this everyone was out to do his best.

I always issued instructions to my team that they should wear club caps if they had them. The principle behind this was that it might intimidate the opposition. This idea proved to have no foundation. The only time when club colours may have fulfilled their purpose, was when a neighbour, wearing an Eton Rambler cap, made no less than forty runs. Whether the cap impressed the bowlers I do not know, but I believe that it was the highest score that my friend ever made in his life. It was this innings that caused my butler, no great cricketer himself, but a true lover of the game, to say to me-

"If I could only bat like Mr. Price I would be the happiest man alive."

Mention of my butler reminds me of many amusing episodes in which he was concerned, both on and off the cricket field. He was a first class chap in every way, but

67

having received his early training in a very elderly household, he had old fashioned manners that appeared odd in a comparatively young man. Once he delighted us by politely doffing his hat to the outgoing batsman, a guest in the house, as he passed him on the way to take his place at the wicket.

The scale on which a country house was maintained in the days preceding the Second World War, made it possible for the house to be represented by the kind of side that could hardly be raised today. I feel sure that this annual fixture was looked forward to, and enjoyed by everybody on the place.

After the war the composition of the house side underwent a considerable change. In the first place there were very few employees, and those that remained were past the age for cricket. Secondly, my children had grown up, so it was to my son and his friends that I looked for the backbone of my side, although it was still necessary to enlist the help of neighbours. As far as cricket was concerned the proceedings went on very much as before. There was however, one big change brought about by the lower age group of the players. Whereas in the past my friends had been content to play a game of bridge after dinner, my children's friends required some brisker entertainment. Several factors helped us in this respect. During the war my house had been requisitioned by the army. When we returned, we lived in it on a smaller scale. Two big rooms, one with a parquet floor, were not refurnished. This made it easy to organize an impromptu dance, and there was also another room available for table-tennis. The large day nursery was easily converted into a girls' dormitory, while the other rooms could each be made to take two or three players. My daughter had the task of importing friends to fill the dormitory, and we had the added advantage of three neighbouring girls, contemporaries of my children, who were available for any party.

All the dances that were held during the Cricket Week-ends were tremendous fun. One in particular stays in my memory. At that time reels and Scottish dances were very popular. One of my neighbours, who was then commanding a Scottish regiment, volunteered to bring a piper. Needless to say, such an augmentation to the radiogram met with instant approval. The party was a great success, and it went on so long that I foresaw that I should never get to bed at all. At 3 a.m. I announced my intention of breaking it up. The younger members received this ruling with at least an outward show of obedience. On the other hand, my old friend, who was enjoying himself enormously, had clearly no intention of conforming when I suggested that it was time to go.

"Well," he said, "this is the first time that I have ever been asked by my host to leave. We can't break up this grand party yet, and I'm hanged if I am going!"

I cannot now remember at what time the proceedings did finish.

One of the difficulties that I had to contend with was finding anyone to keep wicket. No member of the side would ever admit to any experience in the position, and it was not a popular one. At least once, my son had to be ordered to undertake the job, but despite his lack of experience, I do not think that the score in extras was unduly high.

Among the neighbours that I asked to fill up my side I always included one or two of my own contemporaries. Finding themselves surrounded by active young men, these more elderly sportsmen saw no reason to exert themselves unnecessarily in the field. Their disinclination to pursue a ball that was speeding towards the boundary, invoked some caustic comments from the younger members who had to run for them.

Our innings was usually opened by two young relations of mine, whose qualifications for the position rested solely on their own declaration of "quiet confidence", a statement that was seldom supported by their performance. I remember one of them complaining bitterly after being run out by a lad of about twelve years old. He maintained that the boy, in defiance of the true spirit of the game, had been hiding behind a thistle!

One year I issued my invitations to the team in the form of a military "Operation Order". Some of the replies made amusing reading. They varied from the laconic, but correct "Wilco out" of a retired colonel, to an apologetic acceptance which arrived late from one of the younger members. This cheerful sportsman had obviously forgotten to answer, so he took his belated reply to a friend of his at the War Office, who had it franked as having been re-directed by way of British Forces in stations all round the world. I have often wondered what our postman thought of that unusual envelope when he delivered it.

The House v Village match was played for a number of years, during which time we were extremely fortunate over the weather. I only recollect one game being stopped by rain. On that occasion the teams adjourned to the Village Hall to continue the contest as a Darts Match. In this, as invariably on the cricket field, the village was victorious.

Over the years some things about the match altered. As I have already said, the players on both sides became a different generation. After the war we had a new ground; the village having acquired a permanent playing field complete with a pavilion. But one item of the proceedings never varied. Whatever time the game ended, all players assembled at close of play round a large barrel of beer in the Village Hall.

CHAPTER SEVEN

September Cub-hunting

I HAVE an old friend, a first-class man to hounds and a dashing polo player in his youth, who maintained that slow chukkars in April, and cub-hunting in September, were two forms of purgatory endured in anticipation of good times to come. This is an understandable point of view, particularly with respect to the early polo. A cutting east wind can be very upsetting to horse and man, particularly when lack of condition does not allow a pony to go fast enough to keep warm.

The first day out cub-hunting can also have its disadvantages. A horse not long up from grass is seldom a pleasant ride. He is fat, and as he is completely unfit, he sweats profusely. He knows quite well that this is not ordinary exercise, so he gives full rein to a stupidity engendered by a summer of freedom. He pretends to believe that a bogey may spring out from behind every tree that he passes. He peers into bushes, putting up a show of mortal terror by snorting and sidling across the road. On arrival at the covert side the first sight of hounds drives him into a frenzy of excitement. It is impossible to keep him still, so that the rider is soon as hot as his horse. Under these conditions the comfort of the Earl of Ladythorne is thought of in sharp contrast. He, it may be remembered, sat quietly on his cub-hunter "among his blackthorn bushes like a gentleman in his opera stall", while he watched his hounds working in Crashington Gorse. It is even possible that a vow is made to do all future cub-hunting on foot!

Luckily this state of affairs does not continue for long. After a week or two, regular exercise and stable routine have their effect. No doubt the first sight of hounds will still cause a thrill. My wife once had a pony that always stood stock still with ears pricked, quivering with excitement on these occasions. However, horses have now settled down and are pleasant to ride. Thoughts of going on foot recede. The real joy of September cub-hunting both for horse and rider begins.

No other period of the year compares with an early morning in September, which has a charm of its own. The ride through the silent countryside is sheer delight. Probably not for the first time one resolves always to be out and about in the early hours in order to see the day at its best; a resolution that unfortunately, is never adhered to. If part of the ride can be made along bridle-tracks, it is probable that no other person will be seen. The whole world is still. The atmosphere is pleasantly cool, although the sun rising through the mist foretells a hot day to come. The mist itself distorts the view, so that familar objects in the middle distance take on strange shapes. The heavy dew hangs on the thousands of cobwebs which stretch over the grass and undergrowth, giving promise that there will be a good scent in covert.

For many people one great attraction of cub-hunting is the absence of any need for hurry. The fact that there is no question of hounds going away means that there is no danger of being left hehind. Having taken up a chosen position, it is only necessary to keep quiet and enjoy the proceedings as a spectator. The music of hounds rattling a cub round a big wood seems to be better than at any other time in the season. The reason for this may be that one has not heard it for some months, or it may be because there is now time to listen. The occasional sound of the horn is almost soporific, when there is no expectation of it changing to a rapid doubling which denotes the "gone-away".

Inside covert the sun filters down through the trees, throwing dappled shadows everywhere. A spot of red glints against the dark background as a hunt servant halts for a moment at a cross ride. Startled birds flash from bush to bush; a cub or some pursuing hounds slip past; all the time there is something to see and hear.

Cub-hunting is a time for meeting a large number of supporters who come out on foot. It is the period which offers them the best opportunity to see hounds at work. Furthermore the early start enables many people to enjoy their sport before the commencement of their working day. I never cease to be impressed by the keenness displayed by these followers, both young and old. Their knowledge of hunting and of the countryside in general is considerable. Their conversation will contain much of interest, adding to the enjoyment of the day. Most of them live within a mile or two of the covert; they know all about the litter that was bred there; they know the whereabouts of the earths (one of them has probably been responsible for the stopping) and they know in which particularly thick part of the wood a fox is likely to lie up. Their advice is sought and appreciated by the hunt staff.

As the morning progresses the sun gets hot, and on the drying ground the scent begins to weaken. Before long the Master decides that hounds have done enough, and they make their way back to kennels.

The return home is very different from the early morning ride out. It is warm; the mist has lifted and the distance stands out clearly. Frequent halts have to be made to answer questions. It always surprises me that such a large variety of people are interested in the hunt and wish to hear about the morning's activities. One arrives back in stables feeling that it has been a morning of real enjoyment, not just a promise "of good times to come".

CHAPTER EIGHT

Woodmen

AT one time the County of Northamptonshire had
three big Royal Forests, portions of which are still in
existence. Many of the Forest villages have been there
since pre-Conquest times, and they have their own way
of life. In ancient days they were noted for poaching,
lawlessness and general disrespect for authority. Indeed
one village not many miles from my home, is mentioned
in the county records as having "still retained its exuberant, and unsophisticated forest character into the
twentieth century". Even in quite recent years I have
heard it spoken of as the toughest village in Northamptonshire.

We live within a few miles of the old Royal Forest of
Whittlebury. At one time this covered an immense area,
running over the county boundary well into north
Buckinghamshire. Today quite a big area is still wood-

land, and forestry remains the major industry in many villages. I have at different times employed a number of local woodmen, some from the forest villages, and some from elsewhere. I have seen none of the reported lawlessness and disrespect for authority, but I have seen amazing skill and expertise in carrying out extremely difficult jobs.

The first woodman who undertook work for me was Dell. He was not a Forest man, his home being in a neighbouring Buckinghamshire village. He had I think, been forester on a big local estate, and set up for himself when the estate was broken up.

In addition to work as a woodman Dell was a general dealer. He attended every sale in the district. He bought anything that he considered cheap, arguing that someone would undoubtedly want it some day. His storage barn was a curious sight. When I first came to live in my present home, I wished to convert some cowsheds into rough boxes for the children's ponies. Dell produced the complete fittings for four boxes, which had been standing in his barn for years. On the other hand, he was equally an exponent of the principle of "small profits and quick returns". I have seen him buy a lot and sell it a few minutes later for five shillings profit.

Dell was a true countryman and extremely learned about the wild life of the countryside. He usually referred to a fox as "Reynolds" and talked of trees almost as human beings. He delighted me by describing a magnificent beech as a "hysterical old tree", but perhaps the remark of his which pleased me most, was made in reply to my comment on some of his dealings—"Well Sir," he said, "it is no use getting older if you don't get cunninger!"

Dell used no mechanical aids when felling. It was all straightforward axe work. Not that the fellers today are any less proficient with an axe than he was, but when a petrol driven saw will bring a tree down in a few minutes, the axe is no longer used for the major part of the work.

I treasured my friendship with Dell, and from him I picked up a great deal of country lore.

About the time when Dell gave up active work Bill Riley came to live in the village. He is not a local man, but his wife was born and brought up here. His actual business was timber carting, much of his work being on local estates. At the same time he and his team were always ready to do any felling that I required, and they did it with great efficiency.

Bill Riley is my tenant, and it has been a great comfort to me having him at hand in moments of emergency. I shall not forget the night when one of my trees was blown down across the road at about 10 p.m. I had a peremptory telephone message from the police ordering me to clear it immediately, or mark it with red lamps. As I had no means of procuring lamps I appealed to Riley for help. Without delaying an instant he was out with his tractor and his foreman. Inside an hour the butt had been sawn through, and the two halves dragged clear of the road.

Felling trees is to me a painful business, almost akin to losing teeth. I simply hate to see them fall when I think of the time they have taken to grow. However, it is sometimes necessary. We had a large lime growing close to the house which was not only a nuisance, but might well have constituted a danger. I commissioned Riley to fell it for me, asking that it should be done one day when we were in London, so that we should not see it come down. He readily agreed and the day was fixed. On our return home in the evening, not only was the tree down, but the butt had gone, the top and lop was cleared, and all the brush had been removed, leaving the place absolutely tidy. It was as though the tree had never been there.

When Riley retired, his foreman Bert took over the business. He is an expert feller and I was anxious that he should carry on doing my work. When I suggested it he declined with regret. He told me he wished to concentrate solely on carting, and so he would be spending a lot of time out of the district. He offered to put me in touch with a man whom he could thoroughly recommend. It was in this way that I commenced my dealings with the Osborne brothers.

The Osbornes are I think, Forest men. They employ all the modern mechanical aids with the knowledge and skill of the ancient craftsmen. Since they have been doing work for me they have undertaken many different types of job. Clearing stumps on the lawn; felling large old dangerous trees, and what is sometimes an extremely difficult job, clearing trees which have been blown down.

Three times they have been faced with really difficult problems. There was the dead tree in the shrubbery, presenting the question as to which way it was to be thrown. The decision having been made it was obvious that there was scarcely room for it to fall between two shrubs. They asked me which shrub I was most anxious to keep as it seemed certain that one of them would have to go. Actually the tree fell exactly between the shrubs and neither of them suffered damage.

The work which impressed me most was their handling of two elms. One grew at the bottom of my orchard of dwarf apple trees, and the other by my tennis court. They were a great age and had at one time been pollarded, but even so, they were dropping branches. Originally there were three of them, but one came down in a gale. As this tree was completely hollow, the danger of leaving the other two standing was too great, so I called in the

Osbornes to advise me.

They were fairly confident about the one by the orchard. I was told that if I would take up four of the little trees no damage would be done, always provided there was not a gust of wind at the moment of falling. But the one by the tennis court caused some head shaking, as it would have to fall parallel with, and close to, the tennis court wall.

Osborne said to me—

"I will bring a winch and we will put a cable on it, but the tree must fall within a few feet of the wall. I am afraid I cannot guarantee that considerable damage will not be done."

I do not think I have ever seen a job carried out with such mastery. The fact that the tree by the orchard was completely hollow made the timing of the fall extremely difficult. But it came down in two minutes, exactly where planned. Within a day the branches were off, the butt dragged aside and the little apple trees were back in place. The one by the tennis court was thrown with equal success. Osborne gave much of the credit for this, no doubt rightly, to the man on the winch. But between them they brought it down with the twigs of the main branches brushing the brick wall, which suffered no damage. A brilliant piece of work.

It is not only in felling that the Osbornes and other woodmen I have employed excel. The speed at which a fallen tree is cut up, the top and lop corded, and the brush burnt, never fails to astonish me. Everything has always been left completely tidy, holes in the ground filled in, and the fire just a burnt out ring. When working on the lawn the soil has been left level ready for re-turfing. Mud thrown on the drive by the wheels of the timber tug has been cleared away.

Such has been my experience of local woodmen. Maybe they still "retain their exuberant and unsophisticated Forest character", but they are men whom I am always delighted to employ.

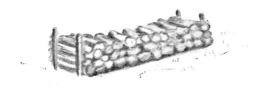

CHAPTER NINE

Anecdotes

WALKING in the garden one winter afternoon, we saw what we thought at first was a dog crossing the Long Meadow. It went slowly down to the river for a drink, after which it crossed the bridge and started over the Park. I said to my wife—

"That looks exactly like a beaten fox, but if it is, I would have expected to see rooks mobbing it."

At that precise moment the rookery burst into life. A number of birds started wheeling and diving over what we now knew to be a fox in a state of utter exhaustion. However, he carried on with apparent unconcern to disappear into the spinney at the top of the Park.

What interested me about this fox was the reason why he should have been in such a state. He was not being hunted, as there were no hounds near. From subsequent enquiries I ascertained that the local packs had not been in the area at all that day. The only solution I could think of was that he had been hunted by a neighbouring pack. This could have been possible judging by the direction from which he came, but if it was so, the pursuit must have been given up miles away. From his appearance one might have thought that his enemies were in the next field.

We never solved the mystery, which gives scope for some interesting conjecture. I like to think that whatever covert he was making for was not very far distant.

*   *   *

It has always been a matter of satisfaction to me that I possess what is known as "a good leg for a boot". In view of the fact that in my younger days, I spent most of my time wearing riding boots, either in uniform or engaged on some sporting activity, this is just as well. On the other hand, denoting as the phrase does, a complete absence of calf, there are some forms of attire where the advantage may be said to be "on the other leg".

Many years ago I was salmon fishing in Scotland with my brother. He possessed legs of excellent shape, with well turned calves of the type required in Victorian footmen. As we were wearing plus-fours and stockings, the advantage was all on his side.

My sister-in-law and the ghillie were sitting on the bank watching us. After studying her husband for some time she remarked—

"Do you know Aitken, I think that Captain Charles would look well in a kilt."

"Indeed he would mam", replied the ghillie. Then, giving me a shrewd look, he added, "But Captain Dick now, he would affront the kilt!"

Sometimes when hounds are drawing the big woods in our area a little Muntjac or Barking deer is seen. No doubt some escape from private collections, possibly Woburn Park. I do not know if they breed in our woodlands, but I should think it is quite likely.

They have occasionally appeared close to our house, even coming into the garden. Last summer there was one with us for some time, living in a wild shrubbery between the pond and the river. We saw him periodically when something had disturbed him. He had the appearance of a mishapen dog or a rather lean pig. We often heard him barking at night.

Once this practice became a nuisance. He came very close to the house where his continued barking not only woke us up, but kept us awake. I went to the window and shouted at him. He took not the slightest notice, merely barking back at me.

"This is beyond the limit," I said to my wife. "We shall get no sleep at all. I shall have to go out after him."

Donning shoes and a dressing gown I sallied forth. Luckily for me it was a lovely night in June, so it was a pleasure to be out. I advanced on the intruder, shouting and clapping my hands. I could hear him moving slowly in front of me, but I had to go quite a distance before I judged him to be far enough away. I then returned to bed and the remainder of the night passed undisturbed.

The next day a neighbour took the trouble to report his presence, under the erroneous impression that he was my private property! This was in fact the last that we heard of him.

*   *   *

I have never been a V.I.P., nor have I enjoyed the

privileges accorded to such persons. Nevertheless, I did once receive royal treatment, and I shall not forget the incident.

It occurred about the year 1915 when my family was staying near Ascot. My sister and I rode regularly in Windsor Great Park. One day we saw some troops at drill, so we went closer to watch. To our surprise the movements were halted, the men formed into line, and arms were presented. We continued on our way not a little puzzled by the episode. It was not until some time later that the explanation occurred to us. We had been mistaken for Princess Mary (as the late Princess Royal then was) and one of the young Princes!

*   *   *

It was on a warm February afternoon that we saw a fox moving fast across the rough grass at the bottom of our lawn. It went through some iron railings beside the drive, and across the Long Meadow. While we were still watching it, two more foxes appeared, obviously in hot pursuit. We hurried down to the rough grass to keep them in sight. The leader disappeared into a belt of trees, the pursuers, after wasting a moment or two apparently fighting, went through the hedge in exactly the same place.

While we were standing there a fourth fox arrived, with his nose down on the line of the leaders. He was so pre-occupied that he passed within a few yards of us without taking the slightest notice of our presence. He too went through the railings, across the meadow and into the belt, still on the same line as the others.

That they were three dog foxes in pursuit of a vixen there can be little doubt. It was I think an unusual sight;

certainly it was one which I had never seen before.

*   *   *

No doubt the extremely hard winter of 1962/63 was the worst we have suffered for many years, but I think more disruption was caused to our village by the heavy snowfall in February 1947. The snow started one afternoon and continued throughout the night. By morning it was lying eighteen inches deep and it was still falling hard. This continued for two days, by which time the village was completely cut off.

At that period, not long after the war, there were not many snow ploughs at the disposal of the County Council, and those they had were fully employed keeping the main roads open. Even a farm bull-dozer was hard to come by, and there was not one available in our village. It was clear, that if we were to make contact with the outside world, it would have to be by our own efforts.

Fortunately the snowfall was succeeded by a fine sunny day. I suggested to my gardener, that as nobody could get to work, he should try to collect a gang who would help to dig a way out. The immediate result of his efforts, was that five of us started at the Village Green to open up the mile of side road which connects with the main road.

It did not take long for the news to get around that this operation was under way. Every few minutes another man, complete with shovel, joined the gang; until every man in the village was hard at work.

It was a very cheerful party that set about the job. A cross-fire of chaff and jokes went on the whole time, and I think everyone thoroughly enjoyed this unusual employment. When we were about half-way through, we came

86

to a place where the snow had banked up into a drift over five foot high. Undaunted by the fact that at one point we could not see over this, we pushed on through. By the end of the second day our task was completed.

At that particular time the village happened to be without a rector. A very good friend from Brackley had promised to take a service for us on the Sunday. He came well equipped in gum boots, having allowed plenty of time for a slow journey; but he told us that he had not really expected to get through at all. To his surprise, on turning off the main road, he found he had a clear route to the village. I think he must have thought out his sermon as he walked, for his theme was based on "the road" and what could be achieved by everybody working together. It was brilliantly delivered, and as most of the gang were in church, it was received with real appreciation.

CHAPTER TEN

A Beginner's First Fish

THE capture of one's first fish marks a red-letter day for most fishermen. Unfortunately I cannot recall my earliest success. It would almost certainly, have been a gudgeon or a perch from the Thames near Bray. It was on this pleasant stretch of river that I made my début as a small boy. Instruction was given by an elder brother, with paste or a worm as the normal bait. I can remember one or two of my more notable successes, but not my first. My introduction to game fish came later. I have a vivid recollection of my first trout which I took on a wet fly from what was in those days, a dry-fly stream in Hertfordshire. Later on my education was extended on the small rivers and lakes of North Wales.

Not long ago I had the pleasure of seeing one of my grand-daughters catch her first fish, an occasion which I hope, will be a red-letter day for her. At ten years old she has lived for the most part in the United States far away from any fishable waters, so she has had few opportunities to fish.

During her latest visit to us we decided to go for a picnic. This alone was sufficient to give her pleasure, since it appeared picnics were unknown to her in New York, and were seldom indulged in during visits to her relations in England. Furthermore the place selected was a lake belonging to a neighbour, which is stocked with trout. As my wife I foresaw would be busy with the eating arrangements, I contemplated a little peaceful fishing by myself. It did not work out that way.

On arrival at the water-side my grand-daughter firmly announced her intention of coming in the boat. Furthermore she suggested, could I not teach her to fish? Seeing that any idea of slipping away on my own could be dismissed from my mind, I agreed.

Interest commenced as soon as the rod was taken out of its bag. Why two top joints?—Was not this an extravagant luxury?—Which way does the reel go on? (One or two bungled efforts on her part here.) How does one select a fly? One thing I was glad to see—there was no call for hurry. The fact that care and accuracy were essential at this stage was fully realised. Finally, with some excitement we embarked.

There could not be a more pleasant place to have a picnic than the lake at Cottisford. The surroundings are very attractive and there is a comfortable summer house in which to have supper. On a warm summer evening one could not ask for more. From the fishing angle it has one drawback—the lake is infested with roach. Large numbers of these are removed by traps, but nothing seems to check their increase.

The evening in question was warm and thundery.

Conditions were clearly not propitious for a rise of trout, but I thought that for once in their lives, the roach might prove of some value. If previous experience was anything to go by a trolled fly should produce them in good numbers.

Unfortunately past experience proved to be nothing to go by. Possibly the oppressive evening was too much, even for the roach. Twice we went up and down the lake without even the consolation of seeing a rise. Well exercised, but not down-hearted, we returned to the summer house for supper.

Fish or no fish, for my grand-daughter, a picnic is a picnic. An ample meal was thoroughly enjoyed by all concerned, but before it could be properly digested, a demand was made for a further assault on the lake.

This time I decided on a different technique. Keeping the boat off the water-lily beds, I took overall control of the rod casting close into them. Success crowned this manoeuvre. A small roach rose to the point fly and was promptly hooked.

Hurriedly I relinquished my hold on the rod, leaving my grand-daughter in sole charge. Luckily she obeyed instructions to reel in slowly, so that in a very short time, the landing-net was used to bring her first fish ceremonially into the boat. Needless to say the thrill was intense. It was laid out on the boat seat where it could be held constantly under an admiring gaze. I decided that the successful tactics should be tried again.

After only a few casts a second roach obliged by getting itself hooked. On this occasion I issued no instructions, leaving the "playing" of it entirely to her. Full of enthusiasm she reeled in the line at a speed to break all records. The fish rose rapidly out of the water, met the top ring with a jerk and was promptly knocked off the hook, while the cast broke with a "ping"! The angler took the loss in the right spirit. It was pointed out that accidents occur, even to the most experienced fishermen. With a fish in the boat and some tackle repairs required, we "called it a day".

Oh the triumph of the capture of that roach! For some reason, known only to herself, my grand-daughter christened it Hannah. After it had been duly admired by my wife it was photographed. Then it was carefully packed in a polythene bag, through which it could be clearly seen, for of course it had to be taken home. Next morning it had to be gloated over again before being exhibited to my gardener and his wife. A suggestion by the child that she should take it with her when she left that afternoon was firmly vetoed. Decent interment was insisted upon!

Once Hannah had been formally buried, the remainder of the morning was spent having casting instruction on the lawn. I have little doubt that another member has entered the ranks of the "fisher-folk". I hope the next visit may lead to a single-handed capture of a roach, or (glorious possibility) a trout.

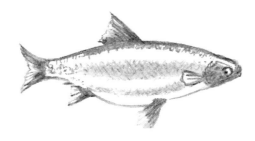

CHAPTER ELEVEN

Grafton Recollections

IT is only natural that hunting people should consider the pack with which they hunt to be the most important one in the country, and to uphold its virtues against all comers. I have hunted with quite a number of packs, mostly in the Southern Midlands, and have enjoyed any amount of good sport and good fellowship with all of them. Dipping into my hunting diaries covering a good many seasons provides me with constant pleasure. It is difficult to write about hunting at all without some apt quotation from the works of Whyte-Melville coming to mind, and one recalls his comment of provincial packs— "some have collars, all have sport." For me the Grafton will always hold pride of place.

I first got to know the country when I was attending a course at the Equitation School at Weedon. Subsequently I managed to hunt there pretty regularly on my winter leaves. Finally, when I left the army, it was to the Grafton country that I retired. I have never had cause to regret it.

In the period between the two world wars the Grafton country was almost entirely grass. It was wet, and often rode very deep, but these conditions usually resulted in an excellent scent. It was strongly fenced, either with very well cut and laid fences, or large overgrown bullfinches. There were one or two really unpleasant "bottoms" that were difficult to cross. It has been said that getting over the Grafton country entailed knowing what you could break almost as much as knowing what you could jump. I remember a friend of mine, one who would never spoil a good story for a "happorth of truth", describing an episode which illustrates this. He assured me that on one occasion he was approaching a great overgrown fence having chosen a place which appeared to him to be weak. To his amazement, as he got within a few strides of the fence, the weak place closed up. On looking round to find a reason for this phenomenon he saw that a well known heavyweight from Weedon was stuck in the fence higher up.

In describing the Grafton country the Bailey's Directory of that date stated—"There is no wire." This statement was substantially correct.

At the time of my introduction to the Grafton it was my good fortune that the late Lord Hillingdon was Master and Bill Pope huntsman. The former, affectionately called "The Bear" by everybody, was probably the most universally popular and successful Master that I have ever known. He loved hunting and the Grafton country with a really deep love. Keen as he was on getting his gallop, he was well aware of the many things that are needed to produce good sport and a happy atmosphere. I have seen him, with hounds just away from covert, leave the line and gallop across a field to thank the farmer on whose land we had found.

The Bear was blessed with very good manners. He was never rude or raised his voice unnecessarily to control his field. Yet his field was always well under control. When one remembers that it contained a high proportion of hard riders, including a contingent of young soldiers from Weedon, each of them determined to be in front, this was no mean feat. I have always believed that it was his own good manners communicating themselves to the rest of us that made his field well behaved. Nobody wished to incur even a mild rebuke. If in fact one did transgress sufficiently to entail a reprimand, one almost felt that one should go home, and write him a letter of apology.

Bill Pope was not only a top-class huntsman, but also one of the best men across country that it has been my good fortune to see. He jumped the majority of his fences very slowly, often out of a trot, and he never gave the impression that he was in a hurry. He was very quiet in covert, possibly too quiet. In some of the big woods it was necessary to be well on the alert if one did not wish to risk being left. He was quite imperturbable. I remember one occasion on which we were held up at a railway crossing near Greatworth. The whipper-in was having difficulties with the keys of the gates while hounds were streaming away towards Cockley Brake. Many huntsmen would have got into a "flap" and fussed at the whipper-in until he was in a fluster too. Bill remained completely calm, never taking his eyes off the hounds as they disappeared into the distance. Needless to say, once we were through the gates, it was not long before he was with them again.

Bill left the hunting to his hounds. He distrusted hollas

and outside information, seldom lifting hounds at all. As a result they would always work. Both he and the Bear were hound lovers and expert breeders. The Grafton pack gave little to criticize under their management.

*　　*　　*

The Grafton country is quite well provided with brooks. The Everdon brook and its branch wind through the northern part of the country. The Kingthorne and Allithorne brooks are in the middle of it, while in the Buckingham area the Leckhampstead brook provides a

fairly frequent obstacle. Most of them have, at one time or another, caused me to get wet. One particular occasion when the Kingthorne brook proved my downfall sticks firmly in my memory.

We had found at Astcote Thorns and run really fast through Grubbs Copse towards Kirby Grounds. I had got away to a good start and things were going well for me until we came to the brook. Unluckily, I chose a bad place, landing well and truly in it. One onlooker compared the resulting splash to that of a 15″ shell falling into the sea! I shall always remember the grin on Bill

Pope's face as he jumped a bit lower down while I was scrambling out on the landing side.

I note in my diary that my mare was not extricated without a certain amount of difficulty. Two of the field assisted me, one apparently a man whom I did not know. Once my mare and I were safely out on the landing side, the unknown, who had helped from the take-off side, proceeded to take on the brook. The unfortunate result was that he got in himself and it was then my turn to help him out.

All this of course took time, but luck was on our side. Hounds killed their fox just short of Bradden after a fast hunt. The unknown and I were with them again before the next draw.

*　　　*　　　*

Following a leader too closely over a fence, is I must protest, an offence of which I am not often guilty. I remember one occasion on which I took a chance in this respect. As so often happens the chance did not come off.

Hounds were running well between Halse Copse and Stuchbury when we found ourselves faced with a typical Grafton fence, hairy and overgrown. The only weak place that I could see in it had already been selected by a friend of mine who was on my right. Knowing that he was always well mounted I took the risk of nipping in behind him. By bad luck the ditch on the landing side widened considerably at the place which he had chosen. As soon as I was in the air I saw him on the ground on the other side. A second later I was down beside him.

Being the good fellow that he was my friend waved away all my apologies as we hurriedly remounted. A couple of fields further on hounds checked. As I went up to him to renew my apologies a mutual friend came up to us.

"By the way", he said, "do you two know each other?" And he formally introduced us!

*   *   *

Whyte-Melville writes of a certain huntsman who, without ever showing to the front at any period, or taking unnecessary risks in the way of pace or fencing, always contrived to be well up at any stage of a run. I myself have never managed to discover how this is done, but I have admired the skill with which other people can do it.

My wife had a most annoying habit of turning up in the right place at the right time on occasions when my son Mark and I were of opinion that she really had not any right to be there. It is true that she had a very active pony, a good eye for country, and if out in a part of the country little known to her, an equally good one for a local inhabitant who knew all the short cuts. All the same, Mark and I felt it was an injustice, that when we had risked life and limb over some strongly fenced country, we should so frequently find her with us at a check.

I well remember an occasion near Preston Capes, an area that my wife had seldom been in. We had run from Knightly Wood to Preston High Wood, no distance, but a very rough bit of country to cross. Mark and I jumped together through a big overgrown fence beside the wood, both arriving with our hats jammed well down over our eyes and considerable scratches on our faces. When I had straightened myself out from the rather undignified position in which I had landed, the first person I saw was my wife. She and her pony were looking cool and quite at their ease watching hounds outside the covert. I heard a strangled oath from Mark, followed by the cry—"Father, she has done it again!"

*   *   *

Hunting is not a sport that lays itself open to a great deal of change. Changes in the countryside take place slowly and hunting adapts itself to them at the same speed. Only one innovation in my lifetime came rapidly and profoundly altered the aspect of the hunting field. That was the introduction of the motor horse-box and the trailer.

I personally used horse-boxes as little as possible for a variety of reasons. However, in the palmy days when I was trying to get as much hunting as possible, they were invaluable for the further meets of the Grafton as well as for visiting neighbouring packs.

There was one particular day on which our plans did not quite work out, although the result was very satisfactory. Hounds met at Canon's Ashby, about thirteen miles away. There were two of us out from my home that day. We sent our second horses on by box with the idea that when we changed, our first horses would go back in the box, and we would ride our second horses home.

To start with everything went according to plan. We had a busy morning and when we changed, the first horses had only about three miles to go to their box.

The afternoon fox was found at Plumpton Wood and we went away very fast. The hunt that followed was first class in every way, hounds running well past Wappenham and Old Mountains to cross the Brackley-Towcester road near Syresham. At this point one of the Weedon contingent asked me how far he was from home.

"Oh, getting on for 20 miles", I answered.

"Hell!", said he and turned disconsolately off towards Towcester.

After crossing the road hounds ran on with Magdelene Spinney on their left to Westbury Wild. Here fresh foxes intervened and as dusk was coming down they were stopped. It was a fine hunt with a point of eight miles and about twelve as hounds ran. At the finish I was only about two miles from home. The result of this was, that I and my second horse were in stables, before the box conveying my first horse had returned. Not quite in accordance with our original plan.

* * *

The necessity of catching a loose horse is a bugbear that hangs over the minds of most who hunt. Different people take different views in this matter. I knew one man who never caught a loose horse. His view he said, was that if the rider was hurt he would not want his horse, while if he was not hurt he should not have let it go. I have never taken such an adamant line, but I had some limits. The rule I tried to follow, was that if somebody in front of me fell and let his horse go, I went after it. However, if he fell behind me and the loose horse came up galloping past me, I was inclined to turn a blind eye.

There was one occasion when the Almighty was on my side. I had three friends staying with me at the time, Bill a bachelor, and a married couple, Bob and Trewly. They all three really enjoyed their hunting and they all liked to have a "go". We found that day at Weedon Bushes, hounds running fast parallel to the Allithorne Brook towards Allithorne Covert. Bill, Trewly, and I all got a good start. We had jumped three or four fences in line when Trewly's horse dropped its hind legs in a ditch on the landing side, and down she went.

Trewly, who was riding side-saddle, rolled clear, but not unnaturally, she let her horse go. Bill and I looked at each other in dismay.

"Damn it", he said, "it's Trewly. We shall have to go after it!"

So after it we went. The loose horse headed for the left-hand corner of the field with us in hot pursuit, hoping to pin it in a gateway. Just as we got to within about 50 yards of it, and were preparing for action, who should arrive but Bob, jumping into the field over a fence on our left.

Bill gave a hoot of joy. "That's Trewly's horse Bob", he shouted, "she's all right and the horse is all yours."

So we left him to it.

*   *   *

For two packs to meet, and join up in the course of a day's hunting is a sufficiently rare occurrence to be worth noting. I have only once been out when this has happened. On that occasion the meets of the two packs had been eight miles apart, so that the probability of them coming together would have seemed remote.

The Grafton met at Turweston, and after an uneventful morning had found in Halse Copse. They ran through Stuchbury nearly to Sulgrave, but swung left-handed short of the village. At this point the whole field was held up at an impassable place. Hounds were running well, so we had to set out on a stern chase along the road through Greatworth and Marston St. Lawrence. As we approached Thenford, we saw the hounds on our right. At the same moment we heard a horn. Our huntsman Bill Pope was with us, so this caused considerable surprise.

When we reached hounds, we found that they had run into the Bicester, and the packs were hunting together. The latter, who had met at Overthorpe, had just got away with a fox from Thenford Gorse.

At that time Charles Johnson had not long succeeded his father as huntsman to the Bicester, so Pope as the senior of the two, took charge of the combined pack. I think that hounds were then undoubtedly on the line of the Bicester fox. After hunting slowly towards Halse they swung back nearly to Thenford. It was interesting to watch such a large pack at work, and the amalgamation of the two fields provoked some hard riding among the younger followers. After hunting slowly for the best part of an hour they marked to ground.

Then followed the business of separating the two packs. This was accomplished in a very short time with surprising ease. The two huntsmen, a little distance apart, each called his own hounds, and they came to him immediately. With a mutual "goodnight", we parted to go home.

*   *   *

The incidents that I have related took place in the years between the two World Wars or very soon after the Second. It is the privilege of elderly people to think that things will never again be as they were in the days when "Plancus was Consul". But this is of course complete nonsense. In spite of the fact that much of the country has been ploughed, and that inevitably some wire has appeared, I have no doubt that the present Grafton field enjoy themselves as much as those who went before them. If ever I am tempted to think otherwise I recall the words of the poet looking back on his youthful days in Leicestershire—

"Were the horses then really so stout and so good?
The coverts of thicker blackthorn?
The hounds truer-tongued and the foxes more straight,
In the days when I rode with the Quorn?

And when we came back into Melton at night,
Tired, happy, and draggled and torn,
Were the ladies then really more lovely and kind
Than those who ride now with the Quorn?"

CHAPTER TWELVE

Charlton Ponds

IF one lives in the Midlands it is not easy to get any
trout fishing within a reasonable distance. From my
home we can get to the Cotswold rivers in a drive of
about an hour. At various times we have fished the
Windrush, the Evenlode and the Coln, having some
enjoyable days on those attractive streams. However, the
distance rather detracts from the pleasure. Through the
summer one would be on the water until about 10 p.m.,
which meant a night drive of forty miles after a day on
the river. In time we began to find this rather a drawback.

By going about fifty miles in the other direction some
of the big Midland reservoirs can be reached, but in their
case the same handicap applies; a day on one of them
becoming something of an expedition. What we lack is
a place to go to for a couple of hours at any time that one

feels like it. It was this deficiency that my neighbour Ronald set out to rectify with the fishing at Charlton, a spot within a few miles of our respective homes.

The ponds at Charlton had at one time been part of the garden of a big house. In those days there were lawns running down to one bank, with well-mown paths all round. When the house was sold the ponds were fenced off from the lawn, becoming a separate lot. To what purpose the house itself was put we were never very sure, but the ponds, in course of time, became the property of my friend Ronald.

There were two principal ponds, the upper, referred to as the Top, which emptied into the lower, usually called the Main Pond. Between them the water ran over some steps beneath a very pretty stone bridge. A small stream ran through the ponds going out through a sluice at the bottom of the Main. There was a retaining wall along this end, built presumably to make the ponds in the first place. This wall continued round one side enclosing a fair sized bay. At the other end of the wall stood an attractive boat-house. The prevention of leakage through this retaining wall called for a certain amount of maintenance, a heap of concrete and rubble being kept within easy reach so that temporary repairs could be quickly effected.

In addition to the Top and Main Ponds there was the Round Pond. This was quite small, but was at times very useful. It lay quite a bit higher than the other two, being fed by a branch of the same stream that supplied them. It drained into the bay in the Main Pond.

One item of weekly maintenance was the clearing of a silt trap which was set in the feeder stream above the place where it entered the Top Pond. After heavy rain this could be a fairly considerable task. The silt had to be wheeled away in a barrow for some distance along a plank path before it could be tipped. If there is anything more unpleasant to wheel than wet silt I have yet to find it.

Beside the bridge stood a summer house, sheltered by a macrocapa hedge, in which we usually had our picnics. Most years a swallow built her nest in it, flying in and out quite unconcerned by our presence. Nearby, hidden in the bushes, was a tool shed. With the passage of years the conglomeration of implements stored in this became beyond belief. However, on occasions when we got an extra hand to help with the maintenance pretty well everything came into use.

The surroundings of the ponds gave evidence of the care and expense that had been lavished on them in the past. There was a basis of good forest trees, oak, ash and horse chestnut. A number of flowering trees and shrubs had been planted round the Top Pond, while at the bottom of the Main was a small group of apple trees that carried some good fruit. On the bank opposite the house and all about the Round Pond grew rhododendrons. These are not at all a common sight in our part of the country as the soil is unsuitable. I have heard that when these bushes were planted a very large amount of soil was brought with them. At the time we had the fishing they were still flowering. How long they will continue to do so I would not like to say. I imagine it is a question of how long it takes for the natural constitution of the soil to get the upper hand. During the Spring the whole place was a mass of daffodils. In every way the setting was most attractive, particularly in the evening light.

While Ronald and I were looking after the place we did not attempt to mow any grass to lawn length. We did however, manage to maintain the area as a wild garden. With a little local help the grass was cut two or three times during the summer, and all the shrubs looked after.

The waters of our home county are not naturally suited to trout, so that it was necessary for us to stock each season. We tried various experiments to decide on the best type of fish to put in, also the time of year which was most suitable. We finally came to the conclusion that 10 inch brown trout in the early Spring gave us the best results. To begin with we tried putting in a proportion of rainbow, but they did not prove a success. At the start of the season they rose freely, but by midsummer we saw no more of them. I do not think they got out of the ponds, I am of the opinion that they became bottom feeders. One very hot summer when shortage of oxygen caused some mortality among the fish we removed a number of dead rainbows, some of them of a fair size. The brown trout did well. There was plenty of good weed feeding which we re-inforced by sowing a number of shrimp and snail.

I always enjoyed the stocking; there was so much to watch at each stage. The transference of the fish from the tanker, the careful adjustment of the water temperature in the tubs, and the final release when the little fish started to rise over an ever increasing area provided plenty of amusement.

Stocking day was also the day for launching the boats, a heavy punt and a dinghy, which had been drawn upon the bank under cover during the winter. In this operation the powerful aid of the man who came over from the hatchery was very welcome.

Looking after the ponds entailed a good deal of work. Ronald, working on his own, was kept busy through the winter digging out the side stream and stopping up leaks in the retaining wall. Once the fishing season started I joined him in a weekly maintenance afternoon.

In addition to the clearing work at the silt trap there was a certain amount of weed to be cut and pulled out each week. The procedure was always the same so that we became fairly handy at it. The punt had an attachment in the stern to which a cutter could be fastened. We used this when working on the Main Pond, but hauling the punt overland to the Top Pond, required so much energy, that after doing it once or twice we devised a different method. Subsequent operations there were carried out with a hand scythe from the dinghy, which I personally always considered a far more gentlemanly business.

Cutting from the punt meant slow progress up and

down the pond, usually with Ronald at the oars and
myself on the cutter. Accuracy in ensuring that nothing
was missed called for joint navigation which we carried
out with commendable absence of abuse! Occasionally
when an area did get missed out some intricate backing
and turning became necessary. With experience, we got
to know the conformation of the pond so well that this
was seldom required. The cutting operation usually took
about an hour including occasional halts to light our
pipes and gossip. Then would follow the most trying
part of the business—clearing the cut weed.

In order to do this, one of us had to go out in the boat
towing a long rope which was paid out by the other from
the bank. Needless to say the rope seldom uncoiled
easily and comments on the ineptitude of whoever had
coiled it up the week before were not unknown! When
the rope was all out the boatman would come back in
a big circle. Once both ends of the rope were ashore it
would be hauled slowly so that the cut weed would be
brought in to the bank. Any undue haste in this movement would lead to disaster as the success of the whole
operation depended on the rope floating. In spite of
the fact that it was corked, it soon became waterlogged,
so the performance could only be carried out once. It
was seldom that all the cut weed came in with the rope.

The next part of the operation was the job of raking
it all up on to the bank. Both of us, at one time or another
had suffered from back trouble, so this stage of the work
was taken with care. Finally we took to the boat again
with a rake to pick up any floating bits of weed that the
rope had left behind. By the time the slimy rope had
been re-coiled, the heavy indecently sharp cutter un-
shipped, and both items carried back to the tool shed, the
moment had arrived for tea. If that tea was mildly

fortified, so much the better!

Sometimes by offering the bribe of an evening's fishing we could induce some young, tough man to lend a hand. Even with help it was a hard afternoon's work, so by the time that we put our rods up in the evening we felt we had fairly earned any luck that might come our way.

Sometimes one would arrive there a day or two after the weed had been cut to find the surface of the pond covered with an unpleasant film of scum. This could fairly easily be removed with the rope, but the job was a messy one calling for two people to carry it out. It was interesting to see that the fish would often start rising immediately behind the rope as the scum was cleared.

Another minor drawback we had to contend with was the prevalence of roach in the Main Pond; for some reason they did not seem to flourish in the Top. They could be a considerable nuisance rising freely to the fly, usually at the precise moment when one had placed it well over a rising trout.

When the numbers of roach got excessive we would call in outside aid to remove them. The contractors who conducted the operation, came I think from Southampton, a distance of about a hundred miles. Having collected the roach they proceeded for a further hundred miles to the West Riding where they disposed of them to various coarse fish associations. It must have been a lucrative trade as they charged us nothing for their trouble.

It was interesting to watch the men. They brought their own collapsible boat from which the net was worked with considerable skill. It was seldom necessary for them to make more than two casts. Sometimes the first sweep would bring in nothing, but the second would find the shoals, and anything from one hundred and fifty to two hundred roach would come to land. Curiously enough practically no trout were brought in. The operators used to be rather sceptical about there being any in the pond.

The Top Pond was quite a bit smaller than the Main. To begin with we tried to keep it for dry fly only, but, for some reason, with the passing seasons the hatch of fly, and consequent surface rise of fish grew less on all the ponds. As a result we came to rely more on wet fly and nymph fishing. Nevertheless, the Top Pond had the distinction of being the scene of my wife's first fish on a dry fly.

One evening when I was fishing the Top Pond. I had marked, and subsequently caught two nice fish of just over a pound each. I reported my success to Ronald who was fishing the bay in the Main Pond. He decided to change his fly to the one which I had been using, while I returned to the Top. About twenty minutes later I saw him approaching the bridge with his hand behind his back, a circumstance that made me suspicious!

"I think this will match up to your brace", he said—thereupon producing a lovely fish of $3\frac{1}{4}$ lbs! This was the biggest fish that I saw taken at Charlton. My own best effort was one of 2 lbs. which I took from the Top Pond in the dark, although I think that I once lost a better one, about which I shall have something to say later.

In some ways the Round Pond provided us with more amusement than either of the others. Although it was very small it had one advantage as the fish were inclined to be active there in September, when they had become rather sluggish in the other two. Owing to the water lilies that covered half of its area, and some alder bushes on the banks, there were only two places from which it could be fished. One of these was a comparatively small rock, and the other a gap in the rushes that entailed back hand casting. As the area to be covered was so small this did not really matter, although the room for manoeuvre when playing a fish was very limited.

I remember one occasion when my wife was fishing it just after dark. She reported that she had heard a good fish rise. I left her to have a few more casts while I started to take my rod down. As I moved off I heard a good splash.

"Did you hear him that time?" I called.

"Hear him!" she answered, "I've got him."

The subsequent battle in the darkness was highly exciting. There was not much room for us both on the rock. However, with the help of a torch and a long handled net a nice fish of $1\frac{1}{2}$ lbs. was eventually landed.

Another method by which fish could be taken from the Round Pond was by dapping. Where the little stream ran out of the pond close under the alder bushes, good fish were apt to cruise around. The method entailed lying on one's stomach to be out of sight, and pushing one's rod through the bushes using about a yard of cast. It was a great assistance if there was someone else to act as a "forward observation officer" concealed in the bushes to a flank. He could give warning of the approach of a fish in time for the fly to be dropped on the water at the appropriate moment. I have happy recollections of playing fish, more or less in a recumbent position, with my rod caught up in the alder boughs, while Ronald man-handled the line with one hand and wielded a net in the other. Needless to say not every fish hooked in this way was brought to the bank.

The Round Pound was also the scene of my "big one that got away!" I remember it well because of the circumstances. I had seen him rise quite a fair distance out for a back hand cast. I dropped my fly in exactly the

right place at the first attempt. The Variant that I was using cocked up in a perfect manner. The fish rose at once making a lovely dimple. I struck absolutely correctly, and he was on. Such a satisfactory sequence of events is rare in my fishing. I felt extremely pleased with myself, but my triumph was short lived. After it had run a couple of times round the pool completely beyond my control, it came straight into some rushes at my feet. When I succeeded in getting down to them in an attempt to clarify the situation all that I found was my fly sticking firmly in the stem of a reed!

As has been said, the bottom of the Main Pond was retained by a wall which ended at the boat house. There was a path along the wall, overhung with yew trees, which rather restricted ones casting. Good fish were inclined to lie close in to the embankment, where they could be observed by anyone on the path. They were not easy to reach. It was necessary either to stand right back so that one could make a long cast along the wall, or stand on the path and make a short side cast into the bank. On one occasion when my wife was carrying out forward observation for me, she reported four fish, one being a really good one, circulating in the area. After a certain amount of direction she got me to put my fly in the right spot. I was rewarded with a prompt rise.

"Oh dear", she cried, "you've got one of the small ones!"

A pity, no doubt, but the small one proved to be a nice fish of $\frac{3}{4}$ lb.

Just beside the bay the little stream from the Round Pond entered the Main in the form of a water-fall. Good fish occupied this spot, but the area was entirely overgrown with bushes. It was only possible to fish it with a very short line, side casting into the fall. We found that by using a fairly big sea-trout fly drawn quickly across the rough water, we could often achieve success. Landing a fish here was not easy. It was not possible to move about and it was very difficult to get ones rod upright to bring a fish to the net. However, the waterfall stays in my memory as one of the highlights of the Main Pond.

After we had fished at Charlton for ten years, Ronald and I decided the time had come to give it up. We had enjoyed it tremendously, having had a great deal of fun there, but two reasons led us to this decision. Firstly, as I have already noted, the rise to the dry fly, which had been its greatest attraction, had ended, and for some reason that we never fathomed, the fish had become more sluggish altogether. Secondly, and perhaps more important, we found with increasing years that the work entailed in weed cutting and general maintenance was becoming too much for us. Reluctantly Ronald came to the conclusion that the ponds must be sold while we were still enjoying them, and before they became more trouble than they were worth. We were delighted when they were purchased by a very near neighbour. Although, I understand they are no longer stocked, we know that they are in good hands.

As I browse over my Fishing Diary I find that it recalls many happy memories of Charlton. There was the afternoon when a phenomenal hatch of black gnat took place, during which my brother-in-law did some very neat execution sitting in the punt on the Main Pond. There was the night when the fish in the Top appeared to go mad! One could not put an oo Zulu on the water without immediately catching a trout. By the time that my wife and I had returned about a dozen in as many minutes we decided (for the first and last time in our fishing career) that it was too easy, so we went home!

I think, perhaps, the lovely surroundings are most fixed in my memory. There were the cool September mornings when the Round Pond was the most rewarding place to fish. Warm afternoons with the woodpigeons entreating Davy to "take two coos", while the sun filtered through the trees. Evenings drawing on to a mysterious dusk, when we would change to a Coachman for the late rise. Perhaps the most memorable moments of all came when the rising moon topped the trees, when rises could be heard but not seen, and we realized that at last it was time to pack up if we meant to be in bed by midnight.

CHAPTER THIRTEEN

A Pytchley Hunt

THE following extract from "Market Harborough", by Major G. J. Whyte-Melville contains advice that I have always considered extremely sound.

"The description of a run is tedious to all but the narrator. What good wine a man should give his guests who indulges in minute details of every event that happened—how they entered this spinney, and skirted that wood, and crossed the common, and finally killed or lost, or ran to ground, or otherwise put an end to the proceedings of which the reality is so engrossing and the account so tedious. I have seen young men longing to join the ladies, or pining for their cigars, forced to sit smothering their yawns as they pretended to take an interest in the hounds and the huntsman, and the country, and their host's doings, and that eternal black mare. I can stand it well enough myself, with a fair allowance of

'41 or '44, by abstracting my attention completely from the narrative, and wandering in the realms of fancy, cheered by the blushing fluid. But every one may not enjoy this faculty, and you cannot, in common decency, go fast asleep in your Amphitryon's face. Again, I say, nothing but good wine will wash the infliction down. Let him, then, whose port is new, or whose claret unsound, beware how he thus trespasses on the forbearance of his guests."

Although agreeing entirely with the sentiments expressed, I, in my advancing years now intend to break every precept that he laid down. I propose to give an account of a run, complete with mention of hounds, huntsmen and horses, although I am unable to provide any '41 or '44 to "wash the infliction down."

One can go out hunting for a great many years without taking part in what may be termed an historic hunt. The Pytchley Hounds have had several which merited such a description, and I count myself lucky that I should have had the good fortune to have been there for one of them.

The Brockhall Hunt took place on December 28th, 1923 during the early years of Colonel J. G. Lowther's long mastership, in the season when he was partnered by his brother Sir Charles. Frank Freeman was then in his zenith as huntsman, with a pack of hounds second to none in the country. I was at that time attending a course at the Equitation School at Weedon, and not unnaturally, getting all the hunting that I could from that first-class centre. Nobody could have asked for better quarters in those days when practically the whole of the Midlands was under grass.

On referring to my Hunting Diary for December 28th I see that it was a bitterly cold day when hounds met at Brockhall. I was riding as my first horse a little thoroughbred bay which I had bought from a brother officer three years before. He had originally been bred with the idea of making a polo pony, but he had grown too big. I called the little horse Peter Pan and had owned him ever since he had been broken. He had been schooled in the regimental school, and had his initial hunting experience in Ireland. He was one of the best jumpers and nicest hunters that I have ever owned. Had he stood a couple of inches higher he would have been a champion. As my second horse, I had out a brown mare which I had bought that season from a local dealer. She had not proved a conspicuous success, but on this particular day she did not come into the picture—which was perhaps just as well.

Hounds found in Brockhall covert, running very slowly across the railway to Dodford Holt. Here they hung about in covert for about half an hour, and hopes of having a hunt grew rather faint. Suddenly they went away quickly and started to run at a nice pace. For the next thirty minutes one was kept pretty busy trying to stay with them. Crossing the Watling Street between Weedon and Daventry they swung left-handed into the Everdon vale, running straight across the valley up to Stowe wood. During this part of the hunt both branches of the Everdon brook were crossed, and as usual, they took a considerable toll of the field. I believe that Frank Freeman lamed his horse at one of them, and changed on to the horse that Sir Charles Lowther was riding. Hounds ran quickly through the large rough area of Stowe wood, to meet their first check just beyond it with Stowe IX Churches on our right.

During the longish check that followed my second horseman arrived. Like a fool, thinking that the hunt was practically over, I did not change. I did not see my

second horse again until the end of the day. During this
check I saw my uncle Philip Agnew, who lived at
Farthingstone, with his coat in an extremely muddy
condition.

"What has happened to you, Uncle Phil?" I asked.

"Everdon brook!" he replied grimly.

As only a week or so before, when we had been out
with the Grafton in the same area, he had told me that
he had now reached the age when he would never attempt
to jump the Everdon brook again, I could not help being
secretly amused.

With a forward cast that has been described as brilliant, Freeman hit off the line on the edge of the Litch-
borough vale, and hounds ran steadily across that lovely
bit of riding country. From then until the end, we were
in the Grafton country all the time. Swinging slightly
left-handed at a good holding pace, they re-crossed the
Watling Street at Pattishall House, passing Draysons
Osier's and on to Tiffield.

From this point onwards the prevalence of roads and railways made the country less pleasant to ride across. But it also made it less exacting, which was just as well. By this time horses were beginning to tire, and there was a good deal less "cut and thrust" than there had been before we crossed the Watling Street for the second time.

Crossing the Blisworth-Towcester road with Easton Neston Park on their right, hounds ran to Shutlanger where there was a momentary check. However, the fox was holla'd about two fields ahead, and hitting off the line, they ran into Stoke Park. There was considerable flooding to contend with in the park, which held up our fox, causing him to double back in full view of the pack into one of the park coverts. Here, in spite of difficulties caused by fresh foxes being afoot, he was killed. The time of this hunt from start to finish was three hours; the serious part, from Dodford Holt on, being about two hours twenty minutes.

There are few things more difficult to get agreement about than the distance covered in a long hunt. The narrator tends to exaggerate more and more as the years go by, particularly if there are few people left to contradict him. I have seen one account of this run which gives the point as fourteen miles and double the distance as hounds ran. Let me quote verbatim from my Hunting Diary—"The point was about twelve and a half miles . . . There was a certain amount of argument about the total distance. I have heard it put down by knowledgeable locals as twenty-three miles, personally, from the map I doubt if it exceeded seventeen miles by very much. Anyhow a marvellous hunt, and one to remember."

My little horse had carried me superbly all through, but not unnaturally, he was very done. Luckily my second-horseman had hung on to the line and arrived

as I was starting for home. I immediately handed Peter
Pan over to him to be led back to stable. As they had
about a dozen miles to go this was a great help. How I
got home myself I cannot remember and the diary does
not record. Probably at the age of twenty-three, after a
hunt such as has been described, this was not considered
a point worth noting.

CHAPTER FOURTEEN

A First Point-to-Point

SOME years ago I was talking to a friend who had done a lot of race riding in his younger days, but had reached the age when most people give it up. I asked him if he still had an occasional ride round. "Good Lord no!" he replied, "I have a son who does that now. My job is to get the horse fit and reserve a bed at Sister Agnes'."

I suppose that is a situation that comes to many of us. I myself never did a lot of race riding, certainly not enough for familiarity to breed contempt to or put a stop to butterflies in the stomach. However, I doubt if I ever had jitters so badly before any ride as I did before the first race in which my son took part.

In fact he was lucky in his first experience of point-to-pointing. He had a mare which was an excellent school-mistress, a delightful ride, and a safe jumper with some experience of racing. She was a good traveller in a box, although oddly enough, if she was going hunting she could put up quite a turn and be temperamental about embarking. When going racing she knew perfectly well what was happening, and seemed to consider that it was the correct mode of travel as she made no difficulties at all.

He was also lucky to have his first ride at our local point-to-point, so he was among friends. This is a great palliative to pre-race nerves. In fact, I have no doubt that my wife and I were far more jittery than he was, and our inroads on a bottle of home-made cherry-brandy, left it in a very diminished state at the end of the day.

It was the Members Race, and an old friend of mine, an experienced and successful race rider, was also taking part. He came up to Mark in the paddock and said—"We will ride down to the start together and you stick to me when we get off." I was immediately reminded of the same thing being said to me by a man who was only a slight acquaintance, on the occasion of my first ride over National Hunt fences. Not for the first time I reflected on the friendliness one meets with in every branch of sport, and the readiness with which an experienced man will help a beginner. In fact Mark told me after the race that he did stick to my friend and that they jumped their fences together until they were about three fences from home. Then my friend asked—"Are you all right Mark?"

"Fine, and enjoying myself", replied Mark.

"Right", said he, "then I am going to leave you now as I want to go on and win."

Which he did!

Except possibly before his first ride at Sandown (in which incidentally he was not riding his own horse) my wife and I never experienced the same nerves again. In fact after a few comfortable rides without a serious fall we became quite acclimatized. So we began to go farther afield.

We had every reason to be grateful that the mare was a good traveller when we set off to go eighty miles to the Hambledon Meeting, for Mark to compete in the Royal Naval Race. This expedition will undoubtedly be remembered as a red letter day by all of us. It resulted in his first win, and the first win is something with which no later success can compare.

CHAPTER FIFTEEN

Hunting Reminiscences

WHEN I look back on a good number of hunting seasons, I find that the memorable days owe their interest to a variety of reasons. Often it is only an incident that occurred during the day, or a remark that some person had made. Sometimes it was the prelude to, sometimes the end of the day. Often it was the circumstances which gave me the opportunity of hunting at all. The occasions which are noted in my diary as—"A day that I shall always remember"—are by no means in every case those on which exceptional sport was enjoyed.

*   *   *

Today when motor horse-boxes and trailers make it easy to get to any meet, either in one's own or a neigh-

bouring country, it is amusing to think of the days when
we transported our horses by train. During the two
seasons immediately following the First World War, my
Regiment was stationed in Dublin. The Ward Union
Staghounds, and the local Harriers were easy to reach
from barracks, but our fox-hunting frequently took us
farther afield. Many days in my diary for that period
open with the comment that we boxed to Kilcock,
Straffen or Maynooth for the Kildare, or to Drumore or
Bective, for the Meath.

Arrangements for these operations called for a good
deal of work on the part of the organizer detailed to make
them. Needless to say such business was never undertaken
by the senior member of the party, nor luckily for me, as
the most junior was I ever entrusted with it. The chance
of such an inexperienced officer making a complete mess
of the plans was considered to be too great. In the first
place it was necessary to find out which station was
nearest to the meet, and the timings of trains which
would be stopping there. Fortunately in those days when
not only hunters and racehorses, but also large numbers
of cattle were moved by rail, most stations had a siding
for unloading animals. The number wishing to hunt had
to be ascertained; the boxes ordered, and finally instructions issued to all concerned.

I cannot recollect that we took any grooms with us.
At the Dublin terminus there was an efficient railway
staff at the siding to help with the loading, and at most
local stations somebody could be found to lend a hand.
We just rode to the station, boxed the horses and took
our own seats in the train.

On arrival at our destination, after discharging passengers, the engine would shunt the horse boxes into a
siding. There they remained to be picked up in the even-

ing by the return train. Thoughts of that return train would disturb us considerably towards the end of the day. One had to keep in mind the distance from the station; a distance that might well be increasing every minute. One had to think of the time required to get back, allowing a bit extra for boxing the horses, and the hour at which the train was scheduled to leave. True the guard would probably "hold it" for a bit if he saw that the boxing operations were in progress, but the penalty for missing it altogether would probably be the choice of a thirty-mile ride home or lying out for the night.

My diary records some varied experiences when hunting by train. There was the miserable time when the organizer, misled by the similarity of two names, mistook the place of the meet. A very dispirited party rode back to the station, there to spend the rest of the day in the most sordid pub that it has ever been my lot to encounter, waiting for the return train. There was the morning when a careless railwayman let the side of a box fall without warning. It came down on the foot of one of my friends completely crushing his big toe. There was the crisis caused by the efforts of a rather inexperienced sportsman to box a nervous horse, resulting in such a calamitous mix-up between the pair of them, that only the prompt assistance of two brother officers on the platform saved both horse and man from disaster. But taking all things into consideration, and comparing the effort involved with the ease of organization today, when box or trailer takes a horse direct from stables to the meet, it is surprising that mishaps were so few.

Undoubtedly there were disadvantages in hunting by train. Anthony Trollope in a well-known article details them at some length. A journey home in a cold train, soaked through after a wet day, was not the least of them.

On the other hand, before the era of motor transport, it enabled one to get many days hunting that would not otherwise have been possible.

*   *   *

A day that merited the comment in my diary—"one which I would always remember" occurred in January 1934. On that occasion it was not the actual sport that made it notable.

For that season, I and one of my brother officers had our horses stabled at Brackley. On the day in question we intended to hunt with the Bicester at Somerton; I rode to the meet, but my friend sent his horse on and went out by car.

It was one of those foggy mornings so admirably portrayed by Whyte-Melville in "Market Harborough". It was too thick to hunt, but clear enough to sustain a hope that hounds would be able to move off in a short time. However, by 12.30 it was obviously hopeless, so the Master decided to go home.

My friend said to me—"This fog may be very local. The Warwickshire are meeting near Banbury. Let's ring up and find out what it is like there. If it is better, my chap can lead your horse home; we will go back to Brackley, pop a couple of fresh horses in my trailer, and see if we can find them."

A call from the local Post Office ascertained that not only was it clearer round Banbury, but also that the Warwickshire had just moved off.

It did not take us long to return to stables, box the horses and get on the move again. The farther we got from home, the more the visibility improved. At the same time I must admit, that in spite of my friend's optimism,

I was not feeling very hopeful when we unboxed the horses at Shutford and started to look for hounds.

Perhaps fortune favours the foolish! Anyhow it certainly favoured us that day. At 2.45 we found the Warwickshire Hunt on the road near Swalcliffe Common, having had up to that point, as we were told later, a very poor day.

Lord Willoughby de Broke was Master of the Warwickshire at that time. His greeting to us was—

"Where the deuce have you two boys sprung from?"

When we explained the circumstances he roared with laughter.

"Well", he said, "with the fog coming down again I was in two minds about having another draw. But now that you two have arrived I certainly will."

He did, and we had a jolly good hunt.

*　　*　　*

Forty years ago when I was instructing at the Royal Military College, Sandhurst, soldiering was treated in a more leisurely fashion than it is today. An instructor was permitted in a normal week, to arrange his programme so that he had one day off in addition to Saturday. In winter I tried to make that additional day a Friday, which meant I could hunt on Friday with the Grafton and on Saturday with the Bicester.

Often it was possible to improve further on the situation. By arranging that my lectures on Mondays should be delivered in the first two and the last two periods, it was possible to get an additional day with the Garth. Of course this necessitated sending a horse on, and giving my morning lectures ready dressed for hunting. This circumstance impelled a humorous member of my class

E

(now a highly successful Lieut. General) to decorate the blackboard one morning, with some neatly executed hunting sketches prior to my arrival in the Hall of Study.

I had many happy days with the Garth and made a great number of friends in the country. Colonel F. G. Barker was then Master. He could on occasions give the field the rough side of his tongue. But he was a grand sportsman, and had a sympathetic tolerance of the young, as one incident I well remember bears out.

Hounds had checked, and the Master had held us up one field behind them. Separating us from the pack was a nice cut-and-laid fence, which several cadets jumped, landing much too close to hounds. Needless to say the Master was fairly rude to them.

I thought perhaps it was my duty as an instructor to apologize for them.

"Oh you must not take too much notice of what I say," replied the Master, "if they don't jump unnecessarily when they are eighteen, they won't jump at all when they are thirty."

*   *   *

To get thoroughly wet during the course of a day's hunting is such a common occurrence that one would not expect any particular occasion to be remembered. However, there was one day that we now look back on with considerable amusement, although we did not think it humorous at the time.

The meet was a distant one. Not without some difficulty, I had procured a three-horse box for my wife, daughter and myself. My nephew, who was staying with us, had a hireling from a farmer quite close to the meet.

Things went wrong from the start. It was pouring with rain when we boxed the horses—it continued to rain hard all day.

I have never liked taking a horse-box right to the meet. For one thing I think a mass of large vehicles can be a nuisance to everybody; for another I think ones horse benefits by a jog on of a mile or two. Despite the vociferous disapproval of my womenfolk, I saw no reason to change my policy on that particular day. We unboxed a couple of miles short of the meet, and by the time we arrived there we were very wet.

I have no wish to recount the sport we "enjoyed" that day in any detail. Suffice to say that an icy rain fell, and a piercing east wind blew from start to finish. Foxes were hard to find, and when found proved far too sensible to face the conditions outside covert. We spent a long time, how long I do not know, but it seemed interminable, on the top of the only hill of any size in the country, while hounds hunted round a gorse covert below us. No one was sorry when the day ended.

I can only think of two incidents that lightened that dismal day for me; both I regret to say were at the expense of my family. The first was the chagrin displayed by my daughter when my wife suddenly produced a pair of dry gloves from under the flap of her saddle, thus becoming the only member of the party with hands that were not partially frozen. The second was when a swinging gate caught my nephew under the leg pitching him off into an enormous puddle. Not that it made him any wetter than he was already, but the sight of somebody looking even more miserable than I felt, was a source of perverted solace to me.

Pride prevented us from leaving hounds before the end of the day. Dusk was descending when we boxed the horses and started on our return journey. It may have been merely hind-sight, but I think I always had my doubts about that horse-box. When we were still about three miles short of home, it came to an abrupt halt. After a quick inspection the driver informed me that he could not get it going again without help from a garage.

The rain was still falling in torrents as we got on to the road. Our overcoats had entirely failed to restore circulation, and wet breeches felt even more clammy than they had done before. It was a very cold cantankerous trio that unboxed the horses in the dark, and tightened the girths with numbed fingers. Scrambling on top of the rugged up animals, we turned up our overcoat collars and started on the last lap for home.

On arrival in stables my daughter was sent to the house with orders to get into a hot bath so that it should be free as quickly as possible for the next sodden sportsman. Meanwhile my wife and I assisted with the horses before following her. Our fury can be imagined, when on entering the hall, we found my daughter who should have finished with the bathroom, still sitting disconsolately in her wet clothes. Apparently she had been quite unable to remove her boots, even with the assistance of my strongest boot-jack. Of course I had the job of gripping the muddy heels and toes, and twisting them about until the boots came off with an unpleasant sucking noise.

My wife immediately put into practice her usual antidotes for the prevention of chills. These consist of large quantities of mustard in the bath, together with a dose of some horrible concoction (the recipe for which I have never discovered) tasting extraordinarily unpleasant. My daughter and I were used to this treatment, but to my nephew it came as a considerable shock. His immediate reaction was to declare volubly that he had been poisoned, and to demand a double ration of rum in his tea.

We then came to the only enjoyable part of a thoroughly unpleasant day. I always think the tea one has after hunting is something more than an ordinary meal. My tastes may be depraved, but I like rum in my tea; I like poached eggs on toast; I like putting my feet up in front of a blazing fire while I smoke my largest pipe half snoozing in a comfortable armchair. I have a special pipe which was used only on these occasions. It is one of the curly shaped type which I bought in Dublin nearly fifty years ago, and when new it must have held about $\frac{1}{4}$ oz. of tobacco.

This heavy meal taken late in the day in no way prevents one, later in the evening, from following Mr. Jorrocks excellent example in the matter of port drinking on hunting days. In fact when the normal hour for dinner arrives, food is a minor consideration. I have always maintained that there is practically no limit to the amount of port one can drink after hunting, provided that there is enough Stilton cheese to go with it.

*　　*　　*

Opportunities to get out with hounds were sadly lacking during the years of the Second World War. Beyond an odd day locally when I was home on leave, I hardly hunted at all. For that reason the few days that I did have stand out as bright spots in a rather grim time. The countries in which they took place were separated by several thousand miles, conditions in them were very different, but each provided me with new experiences and I have very happy recollections of both.

During one war-time winter my Regiment was billeted at Bingley in the Aire Valley. The wool towns of the West Riding have many well justified claims to fame, but it must be admitted, that in a winter of bad weather they can be depressing. Fog was apt to lie thick in the river valley, remaining for days on end; wet streets seemed to be unending, but there were consolations. It never ceased to astonish me, that in a very short time one could be in a different world.

Within easy walking distance of our billets, we could be up on Bingley Moor, in a country of fields, stone walls and heather. A country of hares, golden plover, and grouse in numbers inconceivable to one who had no previous experience of Yorkshire Moors. I have been up there in bright sunshine and looked back to see the fog lying thick along the river valley. It was into this country that we used to go when opportunity offered, to have a day with the Airedale Beagles.

Those few days made happy interludes in what was for me, a rather unhappy period of the war. I note a diary entry to the effect that for four hours I had thought about nothing except hunting, completely forgetting my worries. Hares were plentiful, so the days were filled with activity. I found that I had a better eye for a gateway or a gap in a stone wall, when crossing country on foot, than on horse back. I discovered an even greater pleasure in watching hounds puzzle out a line than when occupied with the many distractions of riding to hounds.

Reading my diary for that winter I find that some of the enjoyable moments particularly mentioned had nothing to do with hunting at all. There was the time when at the end of the day, we foregathered with a party of West Riding sportsmen at the Acorn Inn, there to spend an hour "singing songs and talking about hunting". There was the misty evening, when as dusk was falling, I walked home across country with hounds. We passed one lighted cottage window, bright with Christmas decorations, an unusual sight in the era of black-out regulations. I think the occupant must have been late in pulling the curtains. These are things that stay in my mind when the more serious moments of those years are forgotten.

Hunting again provided me with relief from the war a year or so later while I was serving in the East. I had a fortnight's leave, which I spent in Ootacamund. My main object in going there was to fish, but I also had a couple of days with the Ooty Hounds.

The various stations in the Nilghiris were at that time organized as leave centres. The authorities were extremely helpful to anybody wishing to hunt. Horses were found by the Governor's Bodyguard, and were taken to the meet by government syces. The one allotted to me on each occasion was a first class ride, and from what I heard, the same was true of the others. A bus was provided to take us to the meet, which took place at 8 a.m. After hunting we rode back to the waiting bus, handed our horses over to the syces, and were back in Ooty in time for lunch.

I do not suppose there is any place East of Suez that makes one feel so much at home as the Nilghiris. I see noted in my diary that we had an early morning mist, followed by intervals of bright sunshine and light showers. The country was downland grass, studded with woods and patches of whins. It is true that the hills were both higher and steeper than anything in this country. I also note that at one point, I had to dismount and lead my horse down a considerable hill, locally known as the Staircase, which turned my thoughts to Mr. Jorrocks and the Glorious Old Surrey. The country was not fenced, but it was intersected by a great number of streams. These were crossed by causeway fords, many of which were narrow. It struck me, that if there was a big field and hounds ran fast, these crossings might cause considerable congestion.

Now that my riding days are over, I often refresh my memory by glancing through the books of water colours by Lionel Edwards, F. N. Stewart and "Snaffles", which depict so many hunting countries. It is with particular pleasure and gratitude that I pause at the lovely sketch by the last named artist entitled—

"We'll all go riding on a rainbow."

KILDRUMMY

CHAPTER SIXTEEN

Donside

FOR several years my wife and I have paid two annual visits to Kildrummy on Upper Donside in May and September. They are highlights in the year for us, and it is always a debatable point as to which is the more pleasant visit. Each time of the year has certain advantages.

In May the bird life is more exciting and the spring green on the trees is at its best. On the other hand in September the heather is still in bloom and the harvest in full swing. The strath bears ample evidence of the truth of the saying—"the Don for corn and horn". In September also the weather is usually kinder in every way. In May there is apt to be a period during the first fortnight that is locally referred to as "the gub of May". This may well produce bitterly cold east winds and snow. On the other hand, if the weather is kind, it is very kind indeed, and the fact that the vegetation has not yet become unruly, makes movement on the banks of the river much more pleasant.

I suppose that however old one gets, the urge to be up and moving in the spring never completely dies out. The winter is over, everything else is on the move and one wants to keep in step. Furthermore, on our return home at that time of the year we find that exciting things have been happening in the garden during our absence. We have the whole summer before us and the prospect of another visit to Scotland in the not too far distant future. However, an absence from home at this time of the year has its drawbacks. If the weather has been bad we may find that it has not been possible for our gardener to keep complete control without our assistance. In that case a spell of pretty hard work is indicated. In September, whatever conditions may have been, things are unlikely to have got out of hand, but there is not so much to look forward to. After October, usually one of the best and most beautiful months with us, will come the untidiness of late autumn, followed by the long slog through the winter. Nevertheless, Donside will have played its part. There will certainly be much to remember, and a lot to discuss for a long time to come.

I suppose that in any holiday the journey to the chosen spot is by no means the least enjoyable part. Particularly is this so when it entails returning to a well loved place year after year. This is certainly so with us. Personally I enjoy sleeping in a train, particularly if the train is going north, so the car sleeper becomes the first real step in the holiday. Our travelling dates are fairly regular so we frequently find that not only the train attendants, but also many of our fellow passengers have travelled with us before. We overhear bits of gossip about conditions on many Scottish rivers, and the holiday mood is paramount. One goes to sleep happy in the knowledge that one will wake up in Scotland.

The hundred odd miles between Perth and the Upper Don have never become stale to us through familiarity. The pleasure of welcoming well known landmarks keep us happy throughout the journey. Will those well kept gardens which we have frequently admired be as neat as they were last time? How far will the trees be advanced in the spring? Sometimes we find that the blackthorn, which was over when we left home, is in full flower. This bodes ill for the weather prospects. Shall we see grouse as we go over the Cairn o' Mount? We usually do. On one occasion we had the joy of seeing the hen shepherding her brood across the road in front of us; more often it is a single cock observing us from his point of vantage on a rock, and ordering us firmly to "go-back" as he flies off. Sometimes, on our return journey in late September, we watch big packs moving towards the skyline. Shall we see black-cock as we come to the lower ground by Brig o' Dye? This is a less common occurrence, but they have on occasion been kind enough to give us a good display.

BLACK COCK

Needless to say, it is the state of the rivers *en route* that is given the highest priority in importance. The South and North Esk are duly inspected when crossed in the vicinity of Brechin and Edzell respectively, although we are well aware that their condition will give little indication of what we will find in Strath Don. Even the Dee at Potarch Bridge, although a good deal nearer our objective, cannot be accepted as an accurate forecast. Experience has taught us that there may be quite a different state of affairs over the next water-shed. It is only when passing Craigievar Castle, we see the first burn running down to the Don that we have anything concrete to go by. Finally the first sight of the river itself at the Bridge of Alford either confirms our fears or sets our minds at rest.

OYSTER CATCHER

I do not suppose that the birds on the banks of the Don are really more trusting than in any other part of the country, but to us they appear to be. My wife certainly had a warbler of some kind sitting on the end of her rod for quite an appreciable time, which rather interfered with her casting. The answer no doubt is, that when not actually fishing one is so still sitting on the bank, or having lunch, that one gives little cause for alarm. Certainly while having our meal we have watched a yellow hammer unconcernedly feeding her family within a yard of us, and a pair of partridges land beside the car putting up a courting display for some minutes.

Living as we do in the Southern Midlands, it is naturally the birds which we do not see at home that give us the greatest pleasure, and of these the oyster-catcher comes easily first. In my opinion this is one of the most beautiful birds of Britain, so to have them wheeling and calling over one's head is enough to make an otherwise uneventful day enjoyable. Curlew and tern are also unknown to us at home. Their presence in large numbers

CURLEW

among the oyster-catchers in spring, fills the air with exciting sounds. I have only got one thing against the curlew; his whistle is very like the one given by my wife as a warning that she is into a fish. Many times it has caused me to look up hurriedly, hoping to see her with her rod bent.

The other member of the overhead party, the lapwing, is not unknown to us at home, but their numbers are very much greater on Donside. There we have at times found a nest. I remember once seeing a lapwing squatting in what appeared to be an ungainly attitude. On moving closer to investigate, she took to flight, and a brood of young birds burst out like shell fragments in all directions. Needless to say I beat a hasty retreat, and the family were soon re-united.

LAPWING.

The dipper is unknown to us on our sluggish rivers, and red shanks and sandpipers are by no means common. Much as I like the dipper I must confess that after a time I find his antics slightly tedious. Nevertheless, as the most numerous of the low flying birds around us they are a very important part of our surroundings.

DIPPER.

Of all the birds who are our companions on the river, we probably get more amusement out of the mallard than any. They are of course, quite common with us at home, but it is on the Don in May that we get the best opportunity to see broods of ducklings. I never tire of

142

watching them battling up stream under the bank in the
wake of the duck, or going boldly across the stream to the
cover of the farther bank while mamma tries to entice the
intruder away. I am always astounded that such small
things should be able to cope with the powerful current.
I feel almost impelled to take off my boots ready to go to
their rescue should they get into trouble. However, I
have an idea that they are far better able to cope with the
stream than I should be.

MALLARD.

Often as one may see an old duck put up her "broken
wing" act, it is a spectacle that never grows stale. Of
course one pretends to be deceived, following her up as
close as possible, until the moment when she decides that
she has lured one far enough away from her family, and
takes to the air with a triumphant quack. I can remember
an occasion when I was not inclined to be obliging in
this respect. The brood in this case were not on the water,
but were in the whin bushes behind me as I was fishing a
pool. I could hear them squeaking, and could see little
forms hurrying round in all directions. The duck got into
a tremendous state of flurry flapping about on the water
all round me. I insisted that I should be permitted to fish

143

on at my own speed. Finally she got so worried that she
went off to fetch the drake. Not that he was much help to
her when he arrived. All he did was to fly round in
circles at a reasonable distance from me, while his wife
continued her act beside me. Finally I moved sufficiently
far down stream to be no longer a threat to them, so
father and mother joined the children and peace was
restored.

Herons are not normally looked upon as fishermen's
friends. In fact, in the neighbourhood of a hatchery they
can be a considerable menace. At home, where we have

HERON

nothing important to lose in our little river or our pond, the
occasional heron is a welcome visitor. Even on Donside
I am glad to see him. There is something about his complete stillness as he stands in the river brooding over the
shallows, and the powerful wing beats of his flight, that
looks so deceptively slow, which fascinates me. One day
we saw no less than three standing along the bank of one
pool, on another, two passed over our heads to alight in a

tall Scots pine a couple of hundred yards away. I always have a hope, I fear without much foundation, that the ones I see will confine their attentions to eels.

The birds ensure that there is never a dull moment for us on the river. Apart from the continual presence of those that I have mentioned, the larks will be "mounting and singing" and at least one cock pheasant calling. I once heard a cock pheasant and a cock grouse calling at the same time, which I think must be rather unusual. Occasional rarer species, such as the arctic tern can be seen, but as far as we are concerned the common residents are enough to keep us happy.

PHEASANT

Birds are not the only wild life to keep us interested at the riverside. In May the hares are still engrossed in their "March Madness" chasing each other and leap frogging round the large fields. At all times of the year stoats are abundant. There is perhaps not a great deal to be said in favour of a stoat, but they are most attractive little creatures to watch. On Donside, as with the birds, they appear to be extremely bold. One amused himself by eating all the cork off the butt of a rod belonging to a friend of mine, while the owner was eating his lunch in his car a yard or two away. Since that episode we have never left our rods in a place that we cannot keep under observation. Several times while sitting quietly on the bank, we have watched a stoat jumping from stone to stone just above the water line. It was a most graceful performance. He never put a foot wrong, while every minute or so he would stop, sit up, and have a careful look round. What he was doing in such a place, or what he may have been looking for, I have never discovered.

Nor is it only the wild life that gives us objects of interest to watch. Mention has been made of the "corn" of Strath Don, and to see it being cut in those big sloping fields is always a joy, but the "horn" is equally in evidence. There were at least three extremely fine Hereford bulls occupying our beat of the river. It was a pleasure to see these beasts at a distance. I have always had an enormous respect for bulls. However docile they may appear to be, even if they have got their cows with them, I like to give them a wide berth. In this view I am supported by many people who have greater knowledge of them than I have. As a result I do not like to have one behind my back when I am fishing, even if he is among his ladies at the other side of the field. This has caused me to cast with my chin on my shoulder on more than one occasion. Furthermore, they are inclined to be most thoughtless in respect of the places in which they chose to

146

park. One old fellow invariably selected a gateway through which we wanted to take our car in order to get close to the pool. This necessitated a lengthy detour on foot, always with a wary eye open in case he should resent our passing that way at all. I am always very glad that he never decided to take up position after we had taken the car down to the pool, otherwise I think that we should have been detained there "during His Majesty's pleasure", or until such time as a relief party came and drove him away.

There was another individual, who I think must have been of a cantankerous disposition. Although he had a herd of cows in the field with him, he was apt to leave

them and go to the bank of the river. Here he proceeded to go down on his knees and horn great fids of turf out of the ground. These antics were I believe, engendered by anguish at seeing a herd of heifers on the opposite bank. I felt that he should be left to give vent to his feelings undisturbed. As his chosen spot was right beside one of our favourite pools, we found that we were obliged to keep away from it during some periods of the day.

If the season is kind, we see the cherry trees in blossom during our spring visit. Some of the roads leading down to the river are gay with white flowers, a sight that is unusual to us as the wild cherry is not common in our home county. Unfortunately we do not stay north late

enough to see the gold "that is sticking to the whin",
but it must be well worth seeing when the flowers come
out, as the whin bushes are thick along the banks.

Another plant that grows in abundance is the wild
raspberry. In no other place have I seen it in such pro-
fusion. In the autumn, it can become rather a nuisance,
as it is extremely prickly to push through, and is sometimes a threat to one's back cast when fishing. On the
other hand, my local friends tell me that the fruit makes
excellent jam.

My knowledge of botany is nil, so I am unable to
identify the wild flowers on Donside. I have always
regretted this, as I know that for many of my fishing
friends, they add considerably to their enjoyment. I can
admire the flowers that I see, but except for the clumps
of wild daffodils, I am unable to put a name to them.
My wife, however, knows them all. On one occasion she
identified thirty-eight different varieties in a stretch of
about a hundred yards. To anybody expert in the subject, the flora of Donside must be as exciting as the birds.

For us our arrival in Strath Don is as though we were

returning to a second home. As each holiday comes to an end, we marvel that it is possible for days to have passed so quickly. We are always reluctant to leave, but we find that it is equally exciting to arrive at home again. After we have been home a few days, restored to our normal surroundings, we feel as though we had never been away. Perhaps this is the essence of a successful holiday?

CHAPTER SEVENTEEN

A Nineteen-pounder from the Don

SIZE in salmon is a relative matter. In many rivers a
fish of 20 lb is nothing out of the way, and no doubt,
those of under 10 lb are looked upon as tiddlers. Such is
not the case for those of us who fish the Upper Don.
There the general run of fish is from 6-12 lb and anything
over 15 lb is something to be talked about. Nor are there
a great many of them. Fishermen on these waters are
satisfied with a small and peaceful river containing
plenty of good trout (if you are expert enough to catch
them) with some salmon. Therefore the capture by my
wife of a fish of 19 lb was definitely an event.

Perhaps much of the pleasure of fishing lies in anticipation and in retrospect. Fishermen are eternal optimists.
However unpropitious the conditions, there is always a
chance. There is always something to look forward to,
just as, should one's efforts meet with success, there is

always much to remember. The pleasure of recalling each stage from the moment that one knew for certain that a fish was hooked, to the moment that it lay on the bank under one's admiring gaze, remains for a long time. The more incidents, exciting or amusing, that occur between these two moments, the happier the memory will be.

My wife and I do not catch many salmon. Certainly not enough for us to get blasé about it. In fact at the end of a season we could give a fairly accurate account of every fish caught. Particularly is this so when there have been any comic or unusual episodes connected with the affair. For some reason this frequently appears to be the case, and it certainly was so in the capture of the 19-pounder.

His take was quiet, so quiet that my wife's opening remark was—"I'm into something, but it may be a trout." That suggestion was fairly quickly dispelled when the fish made a slow, steady run to show that the fight was on.

She was using 10' 6" rod with a cast of 9 lb b.s. so the initial pressure on the fish cannot have been more than slightly annoying to him. In fact I think that the light rod may well have affected his behaviour throughout the contest. He fought up-stream the whole time as though the opposition was not powerful enough to make him change his original ideas. A really determined run down-stream at any stage must have put paid to our hopes of success.

The early performance of the fish was fairly conventional. He made a couple of runs to the head of the pool, keeping me on tenterhooks as I knew that there was a submerged rock just below the neck. Many times he moved firmly over to his lie requiring some hard side strain to bring him back towards our bank. After about half an hour of this, my wife began to complain that her arms were tiring and suggested that I should take over the rod. Foreseeing the possibility that the fish would be lost while I was in charge, I firmly refused this invitation!

After displaying these tactics for some time the fish appeared to consider that the moment had come to raise our hopes. Slowly he slipped down stream coming over to our bank. We were nearly at the tail of the pool and I began to congratulate myself that the danger from the broken water at the head was over. I even began to consider getting out the gaff. I was premature in both respects.

Quite suddenly the fish changed his ideas. Apparently he decided that he had had enough playing about, so he started up-stream. Not particularly fast, but with more strength than the light rod could check, he went firmly on. He passed the dangerous sunken rock on the far side, running up into the rough water at the neck. Here he jumped giving us a sight of him for the first time.

By this time backing was showing, and the line was well and truly round the submerged rock. My wife hurried up the bank as fast as she could, but when she got level with the rock the line went straight out into the stream and then turned at right angles. The fish continued to go up, and was soon out of the pool in the rough, shallow water above. The line appeared to be held up again on another obstruction close behind him. A minute later the line went dead. There was little doubt that it was snagged round another rock. We felt pretty sure that if the fish had not already gone, he would be away in a very few moments.

Sadly I waded out into the stream to disengage the line by hand, while my wife reeled in.

"What a disappointment," she said, "he would have

been bigger than any fish I have ever caught. He must have been over 10 lb."

Well over, I thought to myself. But this was not the moment to say it.

There was a wire fence at the top of the pool. My wife went back about fifteen yards from the bank to get over it at the easiest place, while I passed the line over the end of it. Once on the other side I waded out again to free the line from the second snag. This time it was round a small stone from which it ran across and slightly down stream. While I was freeing it, further out towards the other bank, a tail broke the surface. With one accord we both shouted—"He's still there!"

The scene that followed as the fish started down stream might well have served as a turn in an old time music-hall. I was scrambling out of the river to take the rod, while my wife was struggling over the fence regardless of the chance of a punctured wader. A moment later she was racing down stream hastily reeling in line in an attempt to get below her fish. One recalls all this with amusement; at that moment there was not time to laugh.

In fact extreme haste was not needed. The fish was not running, he was at last played out. He let the stream take him down almost to the bottom of the pool. There, after one or two half hearted attempts to run again, he was brought in to the bank. A few moments later he was on the grass. The struggle had taken fifty minutes.

So the contest ended—an event that neither of us is likely to forget. The salmon went off to be smoked, and the No. 7 Blue Charm that proved his downfall still occupies an honoured place in my fly-box.

The epilogue was overheard in the local bar that evening—"Did ye hear that there was a 19-pounder taken

F

on the Castle watter? A leddy had it. On a flee too!"

CHAPTER EIGHTEEN

The Path through the Forest

THERE is not a more lovely stretch of the Upper Don than the Forester pools. One of the joys of fishing these, is that they can be approached by the Path through the Forest. It is only a short distance before one turns down hill to reach the bank of the Upper Forester, but even so, one is certain to see much of interest. My wife and I often think that we have had enough pleasure to make the day notable before we have even started to fish. It is however, on a non-fishing day, when we have time to continue our walk up the hill, that we are able to appreciate the real joy of the Forest.

The Path runs along the lower slopes of Coliochbhar, rising slowly as it goes. On the right, the wood runs up steeply, until it reaches the heather line on the higher slopes of that considerable hill. On the left, the ground drops down to the river, rising sharply again on the other side, where the magnificent woods of Littlewood Park can be seen. Although not really far removed from human habitation, there is a feeling of absolute isolation.

There is little to disturb the tranquility as we walk, except for the woodland birds, and the occasional rabbit scuttering across the track. Nothing breaks the silence except possibly a cock-pheasant bursting explosively out of the bushes to disappear uphill. We find that we continually stop, partly because there is some particular

object that we wish to examine, and partly to savour the stillness. On a day of no wind, that stillness can be almost complete, broken only by a buzzard wheeling high overhead, and the chuckling of the river swirling round the stones of the Foresters. A place of such utter peace is a joy to find in our crowded island.

The Forest is for the most part composed of silver birch and birch coppice, but there are numbers of mountain ash, with some fine spruce and pine. All the trees, on their trunks and branches, are thickly covered with lichen. With the birch leaves, this makes a striking background of silvery grey, against which the rowan berries stand out with a warm glow. Nowhere are the trees particularly close together, so that the play of light and shade between them in the clearings, is extremely attractive.

Possibly the chief glory of the Forest in autumn is provided by the undergrowth. The heather is out, and against it the changing tints of the bracken, and the varied greens of fern and broom, give a mixture of colours such as one sees on an artist's palette. Willow herb is abundant, some late foxgloves are still in flower, while frequently a bank of violet pansies bring a different colour to the scene.

The path itself abounds in small wild flowers, many of which are still showing in early autumn. The things however which continually catch the eye are the toad-stools. They appear in every size and colour. Shades of rich sepia-brown, orange, cream, white, and vivid scarlet make a striking contrast amidst the undergrowth. In the enchantment of the Forest the realm of fantasy is very near, and we find it easy to imagine that at any moment, we may surprise some of the "Little People" playing there!

CHAPTER NINETEEN

Unusual Taking Times

I DO not catch many salmon, but when I do have success it is usually under reasonable conditions. The sort of day when a ghillie would say—"There wull be fush." My wife, on the other hand, is the exact opposite. In good conditions of weather and water you can safely bet that she will fail to score. However, given the sort of conditions in which the local people do not even trouble to go out, there is every chance that she will bring home a fish. The fact that she fishes fly only (with a distinct preference for the Blue Charm) makes this even more surprising. It is a well known axiom that there are really no conditions in which it is impossible to catch a salmon. I always maintain that my wife's experiences in this respect lend powerful support to the saying—"the only certain way of not catching fish is by not fishing!"

Two or three examples of this stay in my memory. The

one which caused us most amusement occurred on a day described in my diary as "the worst possible weather".

The temperature on that May morning was 41°. It was raining a cold steady rain, with the water about two degrees warmer than the air. The mist was down to the base of the hills. The only thing that could be said in favour of the day was that the wind, although infernally cold, was not from the east.

We had been fishing the pools at the top of our beat and were returning for our picnic lunch. At the pool by the car we were on the left bank of the river, which was not generally considered the best one from which to fish, as there were a lot of rocks close in to the bank. However, as we had already fished from the far bank without success, my wife decided to run quickly down the pool while I went on to unpack the sandwiches.

I had hardly got to the car when I heard my wife's whistle. As she carried this for the sole purpose of signalling to me if she got into a fish, I overcame my surprise, seized the gaff and hurried down to the pool.

When I reached the bank my wife was playing her fish. From information acquired later I gather that much incident had already taken place. I have always regretted that I did not witness the start of the operation.

Apparently the fish took close to a big rock. It must have been more or less in its lie as it never moved at all. My wife, convinced that her fly was hung up on the rock, gave a mild pull. As this would have been directly against the fish, it was probably just as well that the pull was a mild one. However, the hook remained firm so she decided to try from down stream. Placing her rod on the ground, she took the line in her hand and moved down below the rock. Here she gave a fairly sharp jerk without result. A second jerk however, produced an immediate reaction—a tail broke the surface and the line started to move out into the stream.

She told me that she broke all records for speed in getting back to her rod and reeling in enough line to make contact. Those down-stream jerks must have driven the hook nicely home, for her fish was well and truly hooked. A few minutes after I joined her it was on the bank.

After this diversion we adjourned for lunch. In the afternoon we fished the down-stream pools. The weather did not improve, and about three o'clock conditions were so unpleasant that we decided to go home. On getting back to the car my wife suggested that while I was taking down my rod, she would try the pool again. I proposed that she should cross to the other side, but she preferred to stick to the left bank. Five minutes later the whistle blew!

On this occasion the fish defeated her. It had taken close to the tail of the pool, and running down into the rough water below, managed to get off. But the fact remains, that for the second time on this most unpropitious day she had been into a fish.

Despite the bad light I insisted upon taking a photograph. Oddly enough it came out rather well, showing the weather conditions quite clearly. Equally clear was the amount of clothing that my wife was wearing. I have been permitted to stick the print in my fishing book, but it is not allowed to be publicly exhibited!

*   *   *

I also recall a certain day in September when success was achieved during the other extreme of weather conditions. The river was running very low and gin clear. Every stone on the bottom could be seen. There was a hot sun, with the tops of the hills in a haze. It was a day more suited to lazing on the bank than fishing. It was undoubtedly the sort of day when nobody would expect to catch a salmon, and a ghillie, no doubt, would have told us that we might as well go home. It is unnecessary to say that it was a day that suited my wife.

There was nothing out of the ordinary in her contest with the fish that she caught that morning. What will always make it memorable to me was the amount that we could see. Never before, and probably never again, will conditions make it possible to see all the movements of a salmon being played. Particularly was this so in the still water at the bottom of the pool. Through polarizing glasses every twist and turn that the fish made was clearly visible. We could see each rock that it tried to get behind, which was helpful in giving warning to apply the side strain required to frustrate the attempt. As my wife brought the fish into the shallow water of the little bay where she proposed to tail it, we could see the dark shadow that it threw on the sandy bottom. The whole occasion was brimful of interest, and one that is not likely to be repeated.

*   *   *

One other incident comes to my mind, although in this instance the elements were not quite so inimical to success. It is the opening of the episode that gives it an assured place in my fishing memories.

To catch a salmon during a snow storm is not unusual, even in May on a greased line, but it undoubtedly increases the interest. On the day in question a fairly heavy snow shower was coming up from behind us. I was standing on the bank watching the back view of my wife being gradually turned into that of a snow man. Then, glancing over her shoulder at a very black cloud which was approaching, she said, all in one breath; "Are we quite mad to go on?—Oh goodness, I'm into a fish!"

CHAPTER TWENTY

Shooting over Dogs

I N my opinion shooting grouse over dogs is the most
enjoyable form of shooting one can have. I know good
shots will tell you that birds walked up in this manner are
too easy, but given a wild day with a cross wind this is
far from true.

For several years I was a guest at Stonefield, near
Tarbert on Loch Fyne. The ground walked was the high
formation separating Loch Fyne from West Loch
Tarbert. The scenery was magnificent and there were
usually enough birds to keep one occupied; but one had
to be young and fit to appreciate it properly.

The ground was high and very steep. Getting to the
furthest beat entailed a walk of an hour and a half
before shooting started. Luckily we worked towards home
on that beat, so there was not quite such a long trudge
back at the end of the day. Practically the whole time was

163

spent walking on the side of a face, which is very tiring to the ankles.

I do not think the size of the bag is of first importance in this form of shooting, provided there are not too many long periods when no birds are seen at all. On referring to my diary I see that there were days at Stonefield when two guns got as many as thirty brace, but something in the range of ten to fifteen brace was more usual. I have had many extremely pleasant days when the bag was quite a bit smaller than that. There is no doubt that two guns is the right number for shooting over dogs. A day spent with a congenial companion and a knowledgeable keeper can be one of real pleasure.

Watching the pointers work, is of course one of the main interests in this type of shooting. I love their loose rangy gallop as they work on a frontage of about two hundred yards; I love the sudden check when the dog thinks that he winds game, and I am always thrilled when he stands like a statue in the heather. Why is it that a point always seems to be uphill, necessitating a steep climb to reach the dog? It is amusing to see him glance back over his shoulder every now and then, as if to say— "I tell you they *are* here. For Heavens sake get a move on and let me go in to put them up."

Then follows the slow, stiff-legged approach until the covey takes wing, it is to be hoped within shot. It must be admitted that sometimes the point ends with the appearance of a lark or a whacking great blue hare. The best of us make mistakes at times, and on such an occasion the apologetic look on the dog's face is quite comical.

I enjoyed every moment of those days at Stonefield. The walk out along the sheep track past Loch Chaorun, and the remote bothy to which a shepherd was said to have brought his bride. The lower slopes of the hill, where there was the chance of a black cock. The steep climb, in places entailing a scramble. The hope of seeing an eagle wheeling overhead. Finally the top with an unrivalled view in every direction.

Days like these have to be experienced, to understand the fascination of shooting over dogs.

CHAPTER TWENTY-ONE

Fishing Anecdotes

THE $\frac{3}{4}''$ tube Stoat's Tail is an excellent autumn fly on the Don. It has only one drawback. It is even more popular with very small trout than it is with salmon. They insist on getting themselves hooked, sometimes so severely that they are not easy to release.

Once I remember my fly being taken right under the opposite bank, by something that I felt sure was a tiny trout. As I started to reel in I turned to my wife who was standing on the bank behind me and said,

"Another of these confounded little things."

"Not so little as all that," she answered, "it is bending your rod."

Looking up I saw that my rod was indeed well bent. Thinking that I must have been mistaken, and that it was in fact a good sized trout, I moved into the shallow water continuing to reel in fairly fast. As the line came in towards my feet, I saw to my surprise, an unmistakable salmon of six or seven pounds. On seeing me, the fish made a run across to the far side of the river.

Hastily I scrambled on to the bank and started to put on pressure. The fish came to the middle of the stream, and then was away. My wife told me that she saw it quite clearly as it again darted across to the opposite bank. As the salmon departed, it released a little trout which was in fact on the end of my line. The pressure of the rod then caused the trout to fly up into the air like a cork coming out of a champagne bottle.

The trout had marks on both its sides where the salmon had seized it, but apart from that it seemed undamaged. On being returned to the water it swam away apparently none the worse for its experience.

*   *   *

Year after year when we stay on Donside we find the same fellow guests in the hotel. They are mostly fishermen, many of them highly experienced. There have been occasions when a beginner has arrived to fish the water, and one particularly cheerful individual comes to my mind.

He had no experience of fishing; neither had his wife. His main relaxation was golf, and hers was water colour painting. The lady's contention was, that if her husband would only take up fishing, she would be able to accompany him, and so doing, would find greater scope for her own recreation.

Aided and abetted by their son-in-law, who was a fisherman, her persuasion proved successful; the husband agreed to give it a trial. They were fishing as guests on the opposite bank of our beat. We saw them on their first day, the lady installed behind her easel, while her husband was undergoing instruction from his ghillie.

I met him that evening on our return to the hotel.

"Did you have any luck?" I asked.

"I caught one," said he.

"Splendid," I said, "How big was it?"

"Oh about four inches long," he replied, "The ghillie told me that it was a parr, so I am writing to my host to tell him that I have caught my first salmon!"

I regret to say the remainder of his visit was spent on the golf course.

*   *   *

I have not often been able to offer advice to a fisherman that has proved of value to him. However, there was one occasion when I was able to help, although it was only in a very simple way. The speed with which my advice was turned to good account makes the incident pleasing to remember.

My wife and I had been having some fairly successful salmon fishing. One evening, when we brought in a couple of fish, a fellow guest who was a stranger, asked me about the flies that we were using. He said—"This is my third visit here and I have never caught a fish. I have tried fly, and recently I have been advised to spin. I have done no good with either. In any case I do not really care for spinning."

I gathered from what he told me that his salmon fishing experience had been on large rivers. The flies that he showed me were bigger and more heavily dressed than any we use on the Upper Don in September, particularly with the river as low as it was that season. I told him that we used a No. 7 Blue Charm, Low Water dressed, or a small Stoat's Tail. "I have nothing as small as that," he said. I suggested that he should ring up the firm in Aberdeen from whom I got my flies, as they could get some out to him in a couple of days.

"I can't wait as long as that," he said, "I will go into Aberdeen first thing tomorrow morning and ask them to give me some exactly like yours." This meant he was going thirty-five miles to buy a fly!

The following evening on our return to the hotel, our new aquaintance came hurrying down the steps in great excitement.

"Thanks entirely to you," he said, "I have had a lovely ten-pounder on 'your' fly. I shall certainly never spin again!"

I am glad to say he repeated his success on the following day. No doubt there was nothing very profound about my advice, nor was my suggestion a very difficult one to make; but the immediate success that followed makes it a very happy memory.

* * *

Cows are infernally inquisitive animals. Should you chance to leave your car in a field in which they are grazing, you can be quite certain that it will come under close inspection. It is true no positive damage is likely to be done, but their habit of admiring their reflections, both in the body work and in the windows, will have left it in a filthy condition.

When one is fishing they can be a real nuisance. Their desire to investigate makes them come close behind an unsuspecting fisherman. A friend of mine was once put to a great deal of trouble as a result of this. He hooked a cow with his back cast, the fly getting firmly fixed in its coat. Needless to say, the animal had no intention of allowing him to come close enough to remove it. For some time they stood regarding each other, the cow taking a step back as my friend took a step forward. The fly was the only Jock Scott that he had with him, so he was loath to cut it off and leave it in the possession of the enemy. I understand he had to "play" his unusual capture for some time before he was allowed to lay hands on it, and recover his property.

Once when we were fishing the Derwent, my wife left her mackintosh on a post and rail fence. A cow, impelled by the "insatiable curiosity" of its kind, managed to

remove it. I suddenly noticed the garment being carried round the field by a bewildered animal that was completely blindfolded. In my efforts to recover it I felt as though I was carrying out the role of a matador, only the positions were reversed, as I was making the advances, and the "cloak" was in the possession of my adversary. From my point of view it was probably just as well that the animal was effectively blindfolded. By making my approach extremely quietly, I was able to retrieve the coat before it had suffered any damage.

Among the host of delightful people whom I have met when fishing, I can think of one who has given me more amusement than any other. She was known universally to the guests in our hotel as the "Old Lady".

I would not like to make more than an estimate as to the Old Lady's age. She had reached a time of life when she was more inclined to add to her years than to subtract from them. However, I have little doubt that at the time of the last visit on which she actually fished, she was nearer to ninety than eighty.

The Old Lady usually visited Donside at least twice during the summer. At one time she had lived in the district, so she had a great number of local friends of all classes. She knew the river extremely well, and liked if possible to get on her favourite pool. She was in fact, inclined to stay on it rather a long time, to the annoyance of the fishermen on the opposite bank. For salmon she was a fly-fishing purist, spinning was anathema to her, and she refused to use a treble-hooked tube fly, or even a double hook on a conventional pattern. It was only during her last season or two that we persuaded her to grease her line, and I do not think she ever approved of nylon for a cast.

Naturally the Old Lady did not attempt to fish all day. She went on the river in the morning only, but in spite of this she was often the only one of us to bring in a fish. She was quite prepared to wade in shallow water, with her chauffeur standing beside her as an insurance against mishaps. She once delighted us by remarking that she did not want to fall in, because, fond as she was of her chauffeur, she would not like to receive the "kiss of life" from him! Incidentally, the chauffeur was also a keen fisherman. He fished for trout on her beat in the afternoon. She said that she did not encourage him to fish for salmon, as she feared, that should he catch one, he would no longer be satisfied with fishing for trout. When she gave up fishing, I think this restriction must have been removed, as I noticed his name recorded in the Game Book as having caught an 8 lb. fish.

The Old Lady had no intention of letting her years limit her activities. She was frequently invited to go out on a neighbouring moor in the shooting season. Naturally her host (and the rest of us) thought of her simply as a spectator. After one of these days, I asked her if she had enjoyed herself.

"Yes", she replied, "I did, very much indeed, but I did not shoot. I put my gun in the back of the car in the hope that I would; however, nobody suggested it."

One season the Old Lady, a doctor and I, had beats on the same stretch of water. The doctor was a friend of some years standing, as we had fished together for several seasons. He was also a great favourite with the Old Lady. At that time we were having a wet spell with the river running high. One morning we woke to find a blustery wind, and rain coming down in "stair-rods". After breakfast the doctor and I looked out of the library window at a very unattractive prospect. The library was very cosy, with a nice fire burning, so we decided that it was no day to go fishing.

To our surprise, and much to our shame, when we met the Old Lady at lunch, she told us that she had been out. Although she had not caught a fish, she had had a pull, and the water conditions by her report, were not too bad.

"Good Heavens", said the doctor, "if the Old Lady can face the elements, surely we can."

We got through our lunch as quickly as possible and hurried down to the river. That evening we each came back with a salmon!

I suppose every fisherman has among the number of "ones that got away", some that he particularly regrets. It was not a fish of mine for which I have this feeling, but a salmon my wife lost owing to my mistakes as a ghillie. These errors were due at first to over-confidence, and later to over-anxiety; two things that should always be avoided.

My wife hooked her fish near the tail of the pool. This meant that it would probably run downstream out of the pool altogether. If this occurred, the first obstacle to be negotiated was a piece of very rough water holding a number of dangerous rocks; the second was a double-arched bridge. At the bridge on that bank our beat ended, and we had never landed a fish below this point. We knew the stretch well from the opposite bank, and had every reason to believe that the river was quite shallow for a hundred yards or more until it reached the next pool.

On this occasion the expected happened, the fish ran hard downstream. My wife brought it through the rocks and broken water without incident, and persuaded it to take the channel through the nearer arch of the bridge.

Now the danger is over, I thought to myself. This was the first instance of over-confidence.

After passing under the bridge my wife got out on to the bank. We reached the spot which I had used previously for gaffing a fish, but her fish was still running hard. Relying on my knowledge of the river from the other bank, I did not reconnoitre downstream.

"You can follow on down", I said, "and if necessary, get into the river again."

This was the second, and even more serious mistake due to over-confidence.

With some difficulty my wife manoeuvred her line over

a fair-sized bush, but about five yards lower down was a large willow tree. Obviously a further adventure into the river would be required to circumvent it, so I went to make an inspection. It was then that the penalty for my over-confidence was brought home to me.

From a point about two yards above the willow, a deep pot ran well out into the river. Any idea of wading round the tree was out of the question. The bush that we had just passed made the business of walking the fish up extremely difficult. It was clear that the fish would have to be landed where we stood. It was then that over-anxiety crept in.

There could hardly have been a worse place in which to land a fish. The bank sloped steeply to the deep water; on the right was the big willow tree, on the left a briar growing out into the river. The space between these obstacles was not more than a couple of yards. In order to use my short gaff I had to be on my knees. Twice my wife worked her fish close to me, each time it made another strong run downstream. It had now been on for some time and was clearly of a reasonable size. I wondered how long the hook would hold. Over-anxiety increased.

My wife brought the fish in for the third time, actually getting it within my reach. It was by no means ready for the gaff, but over-anxiety took charge. I made a snatch at the fish; the point of the gaff did not go home, but the crook caught it under the belly. Lifting it quickly out of the water I threw it on the bank, but before either of us could get a hand on it, the fish slipped down the slope back into the river. As it went, the cast twisted round the shaft of the gaff and snapped.

My wife was so dumbfounded that she never said a word.

When I described the event to the ghillie next day, I was at least able to give a negative reply to his only comment—

"Did she take on much?"

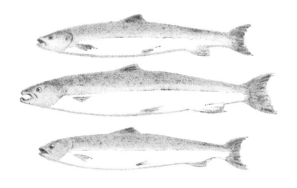

CHAPTER TWENTY-TWO

Hat-Tricks

O N many rivers it is commonplace to catch three salmon in a day on a fly, so that such an achievement calls for little remark. On the upper stretches of the Don we do not expect this to happen. For those who go there, one fish a day for three days running can be said to constitute a hat-trick. I have not so far accomplished this, but on one occasion my wife did.

Conditions at that time were not good, as the river was running very low, and only a few fish had been caught. A very cheerful sportsman who was staying in the same hotel, and had been fishing the bank opposite us for some time, had failed to score at all. When my wife brought in her second fish, he said to me—"How the hell does she do it? If she gets another tomorrow you will have to buy her a hat."

The following day she brought in her third fish, so I

promised to provide the hat. As at that time, her fishing headgear was badly in need of replacement, I did not think that this generous offer could be considered unduly extravagant.

During the week following conditions improved. We all started to catch fish. My wife however, did no good until the Friday and again on the Saturday.

"This is all very well", I said to my fellow guest, "but I'll be hanged if I give her another hat."

"You are all right, my dear chap", he replied, "whatever she does now you are safe—the Sabbath intervenes!"

*   *   *

I can think of another more outstanding hat-trick, quite in keeping with the form on famous rivers. This was brought off by my fishing host.

He is a dedicated fly fisherman, although he is equally adept with a spinning rod. He does not however use the latter often, as he considers the river too small for spinning. On the beats which he lets, the minnow is only permitted under the most adverse water conditions, while on the beat which he and the owner of the opposite bank keep for themselves, it has to be fly or nothing.

At the time in question we were fishing his upper beat,

while the lower one was being kept free in anticipation of a visit by friends later in the week. The opposite bank of this beat was being fished by two men who were staying in the same hotel as ourselves. They are both extremely nice fellows and good sportsmen, but almost as dedicated to the minnow as my host is to the fly. One of them in fact, never fishes fly at all, and the other I think, only as a gesture. I remember once he told me that he had tried every fly in his box without success before changing to a bait. This statement was hardly borne out by his wife, who had already told me that he had grassed his first fish on a spinner with the second cast of the day!

One evening our friends reported a successful day. They had taken four fish from the pools on which my host had the opposite bank. It happened that the latter was dining with us that night, so I passed on the information, which he was not too pleased to receive.

"Confound it!" he said, "I was hoping to keep those pools quiet this week. If those chaps are going to take fish out spinning, I'll be damned if they shall have them all. I have a full working day tomorrow, but I will slip down before breakfast and see what I can do."

The following evening we called on my host to report our results for the day. He appeared round the corner of his house, and when he saw us, broke into a few steps of a reel. This I took to be a good sign, as in fact it proved to be.

"Thanks to your information", he said, "I had three in an hour before nine o'clock. The second one broke the top of my rod, and the bait came away from the third while I was landing it. So, one way and another, I had quite a bit of trouble!"

Since I knew that he tailed all his fish by hand, I could quite believe that this was no over-statement.

178

A very successful operation, but I did not feel any necessity to present him with a hat. In the years that I have known him I have never seen him wear one.

CHAPTER TWENTY-THREE

Happy Memories

A MONG the many things that add to the pleasure of field sports is the fact that they take one to places that would probably not otherwise be visited. This gives one an opportunity of seeing many interesting and often unusual things. As a result the memory is stored with many things, small in themselves, but which add up to a great deal. I have many such memories of little episodes that it is a joy to recall.

One that frequently comes to my mind is the sight of the full moon appearing over the trees at Shuckburgh, seen on the way home after a day's hunting with the Warwickshire. It is useless to tell me that I might have seen the same thing on the way to a cocktail party. It would not have been the same thing at all. Full appreciation needed the combination of peace, silence, and the feeling undoubtedly shared with my horse, of contented tiredness after an extremely happy day. It was a moment when one could understand the ancient peoples of this island who worshipped "the tall trees of Britain" and believe that "the trees all talk together of many pagan things". Nor did the thought of an hour's jog home in the dark detract in any way from the enjoyment in those days when cars on country roads were few and far between.

*　　*　　*

Who but the grouse shooter or the deerstalker sees the real high ground of Scotland under the best conditions? Rock climbers and some of the more adventurous walkers perhaps. However, climbers are engaged in a difficult task with a definite object in view, and have little time "to stand and stare". Walkers are usually following a route which seldom crosses the high tops. Neither wanders quite as freely as the sportsman does. I have not got a good enough head for heights to go rock climbing, and much as I enjoy walking, I do not think that alone would have given me the opportunity of seeing the view from the White Top behind Gatehouse-of-Fleet, or the wonderful all-round vista from the high ground in Knapdale with Loch Fyne on one hand and the Sound of Jura on the other.

*　　*　　*

Few people other than fishermen, see that lovely sight —a good hatch of mayfly on a chalk stream. It is a scene of unrivalled gaiety. Their dance seems to be one of pure joy as they rise and fall with the sun glinting on their almost transparent wings. This display alone is enough to make a day on the river memorable, although the thought that as a result, some big trout may be moving, no doubt adds to the enjoyment of it. It is not true that any duffer can catch trout during a mayfly hatch, particularly if the hatch is a really big one. I remember

seeing one on the Evenlode which was almost too much of a good thing. Talk of a plague of locusts! The whole sky was thick with them, and we had to brush them aside as we walked. The reaction of the trout to this manifestation was to do absolutely nothing at all.

Then there was the occasion at Whittlebury when I was standing in the middle of one of the big woods waiting for the beaters to come through in a pheasant drive. Well concealed behind a bush I had the opportunity of seeing first a fox and then a roe-deer come up to within a couple of yards of me. Each in turn stood still for a minute or two with ears cocked, before moving quietly over the ride and away.

*   *   *

Often I remember with pleasure the sight of a barn owl hawking for insects at dusk over the Test water meadows near Wherwell. The peace of a warm June evening, the silence and the sight of the great white bird sailing and wheeling a few feet from the ground, more than made up for a blank day's fishing.

BARN OWL

Many days after sea-trout on the Ythan estuary have been enlivened by the presence of hundreds of eider duck flying up and down the river, and by the gulls and terns diving after the herring-fry. Once I saw a sight that must I think be very uncommon—two birds colliding in flight. Two eider duck met head on with a resounding clap, both falling into the river. One got up at once, obviously none the worse, but the other appeared a bit shaken and took a little time to get on the move.

Small things, unimportant events you may say. Yet

they remain as happy memories when others of far more moment are forgotten. Would these memories be there if I had never shot, fished, or hunted?